Mary Ann Cotton

Victorian Serial Killer

Mary Ann Cotton

Victorian Serial Killer

by Simon Webb

and Miranda Brown

The Langley Press

First published by The Langley Press, 2012

ISBN: 978-0-9569259-2-3

Front over design © Scott A. Ford. Pictures marked 'DCC' are
printed by kind permission of Durham County Council.
Pictures marked 'WM' are from Wikimedia Commons.

This book is printed on paper from sustainable
and responsibly managed sources.

CONTENTS

Mary Ann Cotton,
Dead and forgotten
She lies in her bed,
With her eyes wide open
Sing, sing, oh, what can I sing,
Mary Ann Cotton is tied up with string
Where, where? Up in the air
Sellin' black puddens a penny a pair.

(Durham children's rhyme)

There once was a man named Michael Finnegan,
He grew whiskers on his chinnegan,
The wind came up and blew them innegan,
Poor old Michael Finnegan (beginnegan)

(Nursery rhyme)

EIGHT O'CLOCK IN THE MORNING

In 1893 a Church of England curate with the wonderfully Victorian-sounding name of Arthur Nesham Bax moved into number nine, Sussex Street, Sunderland. The house had three floors and a basement, but it was in a rough part of town, and it had associations in the past that would have unsettled many people, especially people of the superstitious type.

Curates are the poor foot-soldiers of the Anglican parishes, and they were traditionally too hard-up to marry. This led to some tragically long and frustrating engagements in the nineteenth century.

A Victorian man, especially a man of the cloth, was not expected to be able to run a house in those days, even if he was the sole occupant. A lady who was described as 'prematurely aged' was employed as Bax's housekeeper; the Mrs Hudson to his Sherlock Holmes. Unfortunately, one symptom of the housekeeper's prematurely aged condition was that she 'saw things'. She regularly reported to the poor curate that she had seen a woman leading a child across the yard outside the house. The woman, she explained, was Mary Ann Cotton.

It is likely that Bax had heard about this Mrs Cotton before he took up his residence in Sussex Street – he may even have known that she had once lived at number nine. If this was the case, he cannot have regarded the reports from his housekeeper with anything other than concern. Mrs Cotton, he must have known, had been hanged in Durham gaol twenty years earlier; at eight o'clock in the morning on the twenty-fourth of March, 1873.

The hangman engaged to execute the woman (who should never really have been called by the name Mary Ann Cotton) was an elderly man called William Calcraft. He was one of those people who are as old as the year – having been born in 1800, he was seventy-three when he took the train up to Durham to kill Mary Ann.

During Calcraft's life, judicial hangings had become much rarer events in England. In 1800 there had been more than one hundred and sixty offences for which both adults and children could be hanged, including petty theft. Thirty years later, few people apart from murderers and traitors could expect to face the rope.

Calcraft's life-story is a reminder of why Shakespeare gave the public executioner in his play *Measure for measure* the name Abhorson. Mary Ann's killer began his career flogging juvenile offenders in London's Newgate prison for ten shillings a week – worth perhaps thirty pounds today. He graduated to executions in 1828, and from 1829 he was earning a guinea a week as an executioner, plus a guinea extra for each person hanged. He lived in Hoxton in London, and for hangings in other cities he would usually be paid ten pounds.

Calcraft may have been the last *public* executioner, as the last public execution took place outside Newgate in 1868. This means that if Mary Ann Cotton had been arrested, tried and hanged six years earlier (which in her case could easily have happened) she would have been hanged in front of a large crowd, as the central attraction of a 'hanging-fair' or 'hang-fair'. At that time, public executions were regarded as an opportunity for a sort of fête, complete with stalls offering food and drink, and 'patterers' selling freshly-written accounts of the life of the condemned man or woman.

It is natural to wonder how a man like Calcraft could live with himself, having killed hundreds of people, including a number of women. It seems that the man consoled himself by breeding rabbits and pigeons. He certainly didn't take much care over his hanging work, since he was a notoriously bad hangman. He favoured the 'short-drop' method, whereby his victim was slowly strangled at the end of the rope, sometimes twisting and turning for several minutes before finally dying. This method had been quite usual in earlier centuries, when friends and relatives of the condemned man or woman would often take it upon themselves to pull on his or her legs to shorten the agony. The 'short drop' method had the advantage that it never pulled off the head of the victim: truly skilled hangmen would carefully calculate the length of the drop needed and thus aim to break the neck without pulling off the head.

Sometimes Calcraft's drops were so short that he was forced to pull on the legs or push on the shoulders of prisoners. There is some suggestion that he deliberately arranged these prolonged spectacles to entertain the crowds or, when hangings were confined to prison-yards, the smaller numbers of journalists and other witnesses. He may also have wished to avoid beheadings because in such cases blood would spill on the clothes of the condemned person – clothes which Calcraft and other hangmen would sometimes sell as macabre souvenirs.

A County Durham Girl

The true place of Mary Ann Cotton's birth was only revealed when Arthur Appleton published his pioneering biography of her in 1973. Before Appleton's book, published for the centenary of Cotton's death, her place of birth was sometimes given as East Rainton, or Murton, both villages in County Durham where Mary Ann later lived. It was Appleton who revealed that Low Moorsley was the place. In 1832, the year of Mary Ann's birth, this village, or rather hamlet, was part of County Durham. It is now counted as part of Sunderland – County Durham has shrunk considerably over the intervening years .

1832 was the year of the First Reform Bill, which brought Britain closer to real democracy. It was also the year when a new university was founded in Durham City. William IV was still king in those days, and Queen Victoria was not to succeed him for another five years.

In the 1830s Low Moorsley consisted of little more than a cluster of streets – Low Row, High Row, Back Row and Front Row. It was a pit village, in other words a village where most of the men would have been employed in the local collieries, or coal mines. Mary Ann's parents, Michael and Margaret Robson, were both in their late teens or early twenties when she was born. Their surname, Robson, is still extremely common in County Durham. In his book on Mary Ann, Tony Whitehead suggests that Michael Robson could have been a miner working underground from the age of five or six.

Mary Ann, the Robsons' first child, was baptised at West Rainton, since Low Moorsley had no church of its own. The family soon moved to West Rainton, where Mary Ann's father got a job alongside his father-in-law at the so-called Hazard pit. This mine was owned by the Lambton clan, an old Durham family, one of whose ancestors is supposed to have slain a legendary dragon called the Lambton Worm.

Mary Ann had two younger siblings, a sister who died young and a brother, Robert, born when Mary Ann was three. For some reason, the Robsons had no further children. In the late 1830s or early 1840s the family moved again, this time to East Murton, where Michael worked as a sinker – digging down from the surface to the seam of coal. The family shared their house with two young lodgers, also sinkers.

Work in the pits in those days was dangerous, unhealthy, poorly-paid and insecure. The mine owners, usually referred to as the 'masters', had complete power over their employees, and could throw them out of their jobs on a whim. They could also eject them from their homes, which were provided rent-free by the masters themselves. If the miners wanted to quit their jobs, they were prevented from doing so because they had usually signed bonds which tied them to one employer for a whole year. Even with the bond, miners were not guaranteed work or pay, and they still had to provide much of their own equipment.

The little money the miners brought home often had to be spent in the notorious 'tommy shops', also owned by the masters, where the goods were frequently poor and the prices not competitive, and where many families found themselves running up large 'tabs' of debt.

Whitehead has compared this way of life to serfdom, and it is no wonder that the miners occasionally went out on strike for better pay and conditions. When strikes happened, miners' families would be thrown onto the street, and black-leg labour would be brought in. The Londonderry family, rivals of the Lambtons, would import Irish workers from their own estates in the Emerald Isle. These unfortunate immigrants would be lodged in the original miners' houses while the strikers and their families camped out in the fields.

When Mary Ann was nine, her father Michael Robson (then thirty years old) was killed when he fell down several hundred feet of mine-shaft: he had been trying to repair a pulley near the top. His body was brought home on a wheel-barrow, in a sack marked

11

'PROPERTY OF THE SOUTH HETTON COAL COMPANY'. Ordinarily, the family would have been expected to move out of their home, but the presence of their two lodgers may have made this unnecessary. In any case, Mary Ann's mother soon married another miner, George Stott.

It is likely that Margaret and George met at chapel, since they were both Methodists. Mary Ann was a Sunday-school teacher in her teens, and when, at the age of sixteen, she went to work as a servant in a well-off family, a Methodist minister is said to have fallen in love with her. This was no doubt due in part to her dark good looks, which everyone seemed to notice. If Mary Ann took his attentions seriously, she may have built a dream of a privileged and respectable future on his promises. But the relationship was not to last – since she came from such a poor background, the minister might have felt that he could make a better marriage, despite Mary Ann's looks.

Mary Ann's employer at this time was Edward Potter, manager of South Hetton Colliery and fortunate occupier of South Hetton House. The family employed four other female servants, and Mary Ann may have worked there for as many as three years. The house had a truly Victorian number of little Potters within its walls, but Mary Ann would no doubt have been impressed by the comparative luxury in which the family lived. Mrs Potter in particular, aided as she was by five female servants, would not have been expected to live anything like the rough life Mary Ann had seen her mother being worn down by – haunted by poverty, insecurity, dirt, death and disease.

It may have been at South Hetton House that Mary Ann Robson met her friend Margaret Cotton, a fellow-servant who had come north from Wisbech in Cambridgeshire. As can perhaps be guessed from Margaret's surname, this friendship was to have dire consequences for the Cotton family in years to come.

The Methodist minister was not, of course, the only man to notice Mary Ann. Some time late in 1851 or early in 1852, the unmarried girl fell pregnant, probably by the man she was to marry in July 1852, a miner called William Mowbray. Although such 'shotgun' weddings have always been common enough, the circumstances surrounding this one were still likely to have shocked the members of Mary Ann's Methodist family. The couple got married in what must have been practically a secret ceremony, miles away at a register office (not a church) in Newcastle. Whitehead suggests that they lied to the registrar about living in Westgate in Newcastle itself. This was by no means the last time that Mary Ann would lie to officials.

Unable, perhaps, to bear the wagging tongues of their neighbours in County Durham, the young couple fled almost as far from the north-east as they could go without actually leaving England. They lived for several years in the south-west; perhaps in Plymouth; in Penzance, and almost certainly at St Germans in Cornwall. William Mowbray worked for a railway contractor, and here, two days' train-ride from Mary Ann's home, the Mowbrays could at least pretend that they had been married a little before the new Mrs Mowbray became pregnant.

We know about the St Germans link because Whitehead, while researching his book on Mary Ann, discovered a birth certificate for a Margaret Jane Mowbray, born in June 1856 at St Germans, to a Mary Ann Mowbray, 'formerly Robson'. Margaret Jane was the last of four or five children born to Mary Ann in the south-west, and the only one to survive long enough to leave the south-west with her parents. This information was coaxed out of their mother after her arrest, and practically nothing more is known about Margaret Jane's unfortunate older siblings. Given the later accusations that were made against their mother, it is tempting to include these children in the tally of their mother's murders, but there is no evidence to support this.

Whitehead paints a colourful picture of the life the Mowbray family might have lived in the south-west, living in tents or demountable huts alongside the railway as it was being built, and mixing with those Irish supermen, the navigators or 'navvies' who laid out the metal veins of England's new transport system. In such conditions, the Mowbrays' first children could have died of any number of diseases, or even in accidents. In those days health and safety (especially the health and safety of working-class children) was not much thought of.

13

It did not escape Appleton's attention that by moving to the south-west of England, Mary Ann was placing herself at the heart of arsenic production in England. As Whorton tells us in his book *Arsenic century*, about half the arsenic used throughout the world in Victorian times came from Devon and Cornwall. As the copper mines began to run out of copper, companies like the Devonshire Great Consolidated Copper Mining Company began to refine arsenic out of the waste-heaps around the mines. With so much arsenic about, the temptations for poisoners must have been irresistible. In the year after Mary Ann's death, a disgruntled employee of the West of England Arsenic Works poisoned two hundred of his fellow-workers by putting arsenic into a drinking-water tank.

In areas near such plants, the effects of arsenic, for instance on farm-animals and the local population (particularly some of those who worked in the plants) would have been plain to see. Did Mary Ann Mowbray first learn the uses of arsenic near the source of most of the arsenic in England?

The fact that the last of the Mowbrays' children to be born in the south-west had her Christian name may have persuaded Mary Ann's mother, now called Margaret Stott, to make the two-day journey and visit her new granddaughter. Soon after this visit, which may have been part of a reconciliation between Mary Ann and her family, the Mowbrays moved back up north with their only surviving child.

The Stotts, the Mowbrays and Mary Ann's brother Robert were now all living at South Hetton. Although he still worked in the mines, Mary Ann's step-father George Stott also ran a public house there, and it seems that his step-daughter now lived above the pub, which may have been called the Butcher's Arms or the Screener's Arms. Here Mary Ann gave birth to a daughter, Isabella, in September 1858.

It was in this home above a public house that the Mowbray's surviving daughter born in Cornwall, Margaret Jane, died, at the age of four, of 'scarletina anginosa and exhaustion' after a fifteen-day illness. The details of the death came to light when Tony Whitehead found the relevant death certificate.

Although no details have yet come to light of the children lost to the Mowbrays in the south-west of England, little Margaret Jane's death certificate would seem to prove that she was not poisoned, or that poison, if administered, was not the only cause of her death. Scarletina was pretty common among the mining communities of those days, and it it unlikely that the forty-year old colliery doctor Samuel Broadbent, who made the diagnosis, could have mistaken the symptoms of arsenic poisoning for scarletina, which leaves a distinctive rash on the skin.

Mary Ann never seems to have had any problems getting pregnant, and ten months after the death of the first Margaret Jane another Margaret Jane was born at South Hetton. The Mowbrays soon moved to Hendon in Sunderland, however, when Mary Ann's husband got a job as a stoker on a steam-ship. It was at Hendon that a son, John, was born to Mary Ann in July 1863.

Sunderland was a classic Victorian boom town but, as we shall see, house-building could not keep up with the expansion of its population, so that overcrowding became a serious threat to public health. Although the nearby coal-mines were an important source of employment for the men of Sunderland, in 1861 over a quarter of men over the age of twenty in the town worked at sea.

The maritime equivalent of the bond that miners had to sign up to was the ship's articles – breaking these could land a sailor in gaol for ninety days. Merchant ships were often poorly-built, and their hazardousness was increased by the dangerous overloading demanded by unscrupulous owners. Sometimes these owners made a profit if a ship went down, because, like some of Mary Ann Cotton's victims, the ships were insured.

According to George Patterson in an article in Milburn and Miller's history of modern Sunderland, overloading also meant that the sailors lived in very cramped conditions, in 'an overcrowded, unventilated, leaky and verminous foc'sle', eating food that was 'often old, foul and inadequate, as owners, captains and suppliers all cheated to line their pockets'. Whatever conditions Mary Ann encountered in Hendon, they could hardly have been as bad as those endured by her husband, for the sake of a pathetic wage, at sea.

Mary Ann had now been married to William Mowbray for eleven

years, and had had as many as eight children by him – the four or five born in the south-west (including the first Margaret Jane); Isabella, the second Margaret Jane, and John. The last three of these lived for a time with Mary Ann at Hendon, but soon one of them, little John, was dead at just over a year old. He was registered as having died of diarrhoea, which is a symptom of arsenic poisoning.

Because We Are Too Many

Whitehead believed that it was with the death of little John Mowbray, when Mary Ann was about thirty-one years of age, that the girl from Low Moorsley began her career as a poisoner. He suggests that she had motive, in that she had begun an extra-marital affair with a local miner called Joseph Nattrass, a red-headed man who was several years her junior. Mary Ann may or may not have known that Nattrass was married. Young John Mowbray may have got in the way of Mary Ann's trysts with her lover. Her two daughters were around five and three years old at this time, and it may have been possible to 'dump' them with a friend or relative while she went to see Nattrass. This would have been more difficult with a tiny infant.

John's death was 'covered' by the Prudential insurance company, and his mother would have received a small pay-out when she presented the Prudential with the death certificate.

Mary Ann had opportunity for both murder and adultery because her husband the stoker was often away at sea. She would surely have expanded her opportunities for assignations with Joseph Nattrass by ridding herself of her tiny son.

Hendon, the area of Sunderland where Mary Ann now lived, was notorious at the time as a sleazy waterside district, with its share of drunkards, prostitutes and criminals. In such a place infanticide, which Mary Ann may now have committed, would not have been unknown. The killing of unwanted children has been happening since ancient times, when deformed or illegitimate Roman babies were exposed on hillsides, or left in baskets at the ends of city streets. Infanticide is known to happen even today in parts of the developing world, where, in some cases, girls are killed because parents would prefer to try again – for a boy.

In Victorian England, where poverty was endemic, birth-control little understood and abortion illegal, many resorted to infanticide. Whorton tells us that in 1849 a Wiltshire woman called Rebecca Smith killed eight of her children because she feared that otherwise they would starve to death, their father being a feckless alcoholic. The rise in the availability of life-insurance in the nineteenth century provided another motive: this was understood by Parliament, which passed a law in 1850 forbidding anyone to insure a child under ten for more than three pounds.

Thomas Hardy's gruelling 1895 novel *Jude the Obscure* includes a fictional account of a child killing his two step-siblings and himself, leaving a note explaining that he had done this 'because we are too menny'.

Arsenic was ideally suited to infanticide since it was available to women in those days in the ingredients of many household products, and its effects were similar to the effects of familiar gastric diseases, including typhoid, which killed many children at the time. Few Victorian doctors would have looked askance at a baby that died of anything like typhoid, especially the baby of a poor woman living in a place like Hendon.

It is possible, of course, that John was actually Joseph Nattrass's son. It may be that at fourteen months the boy was starting to look a little like Nattrass, a man who could easily have been known to Mary Ann's husband and to other members of her family.

The two girls aside, the greatest impediment to Mary Ann's affair with Nattrass would now have been her husband William. The fact that William Mowbray died in Hendon just four months after little John looks very suspicious, given the context. But Mowbray, it would seem, was not poisoned. His death certificate reveals that he died of typhus, a disease which, to an experienced doctor, could not be confused with typhoid or with arsenic poisoning.

The fact that Mowbray died of typhus speaks volumes about the conditions in which he lived and worked. Typhus is spread by lice in filthy, overcrowded conditions, such as Mowbray may have encountered on board ship, and perhaps even at home. It leaves distinctive red marks on the skin and is also known as 'gaol-fever' because it was common in such places as London's Newgate Prison, where at times thousands of dead lice crunched underfoot like gravel.

Hendon was not the only place in Sunderland to have unhealthy conditions. In Milburn and Miller's book, T.H. Corfe tells us that in Sunderland parish in 1851 there were on average around ten people to every house. With perhaps nineteen thousand people in the overcrowded parish, each person had some thirty-eight square yards to live in. Fewer than seven percent of the houses had their own toilets, and those who had to venture abroad for relief often used stinking middens and pools. The inevitable stench was enhanced by the presence of pigs kept by the locals for fattening. There were many pubs and slaughter-houses, and in many places lighting and drainage were very poor.

Since Mowbray's typhus ended with two days of diarrhoea, it may be that, seeing that her husband was sickening, Mary Ann slipped some arsenic into his food, drink or medicine and thus gave him the final push into his grave. This practice of deliberately worsening an existing condition would make it more difficult for the authorities to detect murder. As wives are supposed to help their husbands, in the words of the marriage service, 'in sickness and in health', the murderous spouse could administer poison while appearing to be a ministering angel; a Florence Nightingale with a skull, as it were, instead of a lamp.

Just months after the death of her father from typhus, the second Margaret Jane Mowbray succumbed to the same disease, in April 1865, aged only three and a half. By this time, Mary Ann had moved from Hendon to Seaham. Her last surviving child at this time, six year-old Isabella, was sent to live with her maternal grandmother, Mary Ann's own mother Margaret. It has been suggested that Mary Ann, now alone, could have taken up a career in prostitution at this time, soliciting sailors in Seaham, an important coal port. She could also have worked as a dress-maker or a nurse. It may be that she had to break off her affair with Joseph Nattrass, because he moved away to Shildon in search of work, accompanied by his wife Catherine.

Although two members of her family had just died of a disease associated with extreme dirtiness, Mary Ann found work as a 'fever nurse' at the Sunderland Infirmary shortly after she moved back to that town later in 1865. This does not, of course, mean that Mary Ann Cotton received extensive training in nursing. Despite the reforms being introduced by the famous Florence Nightingale, most English nurses in the 1860s were still little more than domestic servants who happened to be employed in a hospital. They cleaned, dispensed medicines, changed dressings and generally helped out, but they had nothing like the skills and knowledge deployed by modern nurses. For this hard and dangerous work Mary Ann was paid five shillings a day – equivalent to about four pounds in modern money.

The Infirmary itself had been built between 1822 and 1824. Designed by the noted Durham architect Ignatius Bonomi, it still stands today, though in a somewhat altered form. The building was not used as a hospital after 1867, but it had been built to house sixty beds, of which twenty were for fever victims.

Some have speculated that it was at the Sunderland Infirmary that Mary Ann Cotton first came into contact with poisons such as arsenic, which would have been kept in the hospital's dispensary and used as medicines. It is unlikely that Mary Ann would have encountered poison for the *first* time there, as it was easy to pick up such substances in ordinary shops in those days. In any case Mary Ann had probably poisoned at least one of her victims before she started earning money as a nurse.

It is possible that Mary Ann poisoned some of the patients at the Infirmary, but there is no direct evidence of this. As we shall see in the notorious case of Marie Madeleine de Brinvilliers, a hospital could serve as a good testing-ground for a poisoner's skill. Before the advent of the modern hospital, death was far more common in such places, and the authorities might not have had the will or the resources to mount an in-depth investigation of every fatality. Inmates were 'labelled' as having a particular disease, perhaps before they even entered the hospital, and nobody would be surprised if a typhoid patient died of typhoid-like symptoms.

Mary Ann was now a widow in her early thirties, and it seems that she had not lost all of her good looks, despite a hard life and much child-bearing.

There is a tendency for men to fall in love with the nurses who look after them in hospital – something that most nurses take in their stride. At Sunderland Infirmary a patient called George Ward fell for Mary Ann's dark looks and they were soon married, at St Peter's in nearby Monkwearmouth, on the 28th of August. The year was still 1865, and the fact that Mary Ann had married again so quickly after the recent deaths in her family might explain why there seems not to have been any family present at the ceremony.

The bloom of hospital romance quickly faded from Mary Ann's marriage to George Ward. His new wife had left her nursing job and was now keeping house for him. The new husband was soon ill again, however, and unable to earn money. For several months the Wards lived on four shillings a week parish relief. Mary Ann was now worse off than when she had been working as an untrained nurse, because then she was earning perhaps five or six shillings a week, and had only herself to feed.

George Ward soon began to get seriously ill. His symptoms included general weakness, nosebleeds, paralysis of the hands and feet, and a swollen liver. He was attended by three doctors – Maling, Gammage and Dixon: Maling was house-surgeon at the hospital where Mary Ann had worked. Dixon suggested that Mary Ann apply leeches to Ward's swollen liver.

The medicinal use of leeches goes back to the time of the Ancient Egyptians, and in Medieval England medics used them so often that the word 'leech' was frequently used as a synonym for 'doctor'. One drawback of their use is that patients tend to find the whole procedure disgusting. As she supervised her ailing husband's case, Mary Ann may have tried to tap into this natural revulsion by blaming Dr Dixon's leeches for making George worse. A formal complaint was made against Dixon, which was even covered in the local newspaper, but he was later completely exonerated.

If George Ward was dying from arsenic poisoning when the leeches were applied to him, then it is possible that his doctors missed an important clue. If one or more of these parasitic creatures had died soon after drinking Ward's blood, then that might have indicated the presence of poison. In a French case reported in the *Lancet* in 1825, the death of leeches applied to the victim was taken as evidence against a Madame Laurent, who stood accused of poisoning her husband. The eminent toxicologist Mathieu Orfila was called in as an expert witness in this case, and he devised a macabre experiment to test the theory about the leeches dying after a meal of poisoned blood. Orfila poisoned a dog with arsenic, applied leeches to it and noted that they all died within four days. In this case the accused was, however, acquitted, since no arsenic was conclusively proven to have been been present in the body of the supposed victim.

Whether he was poisoned or not, George Ward took a long time to die: he finally gave up the ghost in October 1866, fourteen months after his wedding to Mary Ann. He was thirty-three. His death certificate states that he died of 'English Cholera and Typhoid Fever': arsenic could certainly mimic the actions of both of these diseases.

THE HOUSEKEEPER

Just two months after the death of her second husband, Mary Ann Ward, as she now was, landed a job in the household of James Robinson, of Grace Street, Pallion, Sunderland.

Robinson was a widower with five children. He was rather better-off than either of Mary Ann's deceased husbands had been – he was a maker of ships; a shipyard foreman.

Shipbuilding in Sunderland dates back to the fourteenth century, and by the nineteenth century the town, which had originally been noted as a busy coal port, became the biggest ship-building centre in the world. Thousands of local people worked in this industry, and James Robinson of Grace Street, Pallion was one of them.

The position Mary Ann Ward won in James's household was that of live-in housekeeper. As such, she would have been responsible for many of the household duties that would previously have been carried out by Robinson's wife, the late Hannah Robinson, née Greenwell.

The youngest of Hannah and James's children was little John, who was only nine months old when Mary Ann came into the house at Pallion. The day after Mary Ann arrived to take up the position of live-in housekeeper, little John Robinson was dead of convulsions, which could have been a symptom of arsenic poisoning.

Whitehead believed that Mary Ann would not have poisoned the baby so quickly after entering the house, but he did believe that she poisoned her own son, also called John, just over a year after his birth in 1863. It may be that the new housekeeper was given the baby to look after and that she immediately found this an intolerable imposition. She may have intended to kill the child by slow poisoning to simulate a lengthy illness, as she had probably done before in the case of her second husband. The baby may have died more quickly than she intended, because the action of arsenic is unpredictable, and its effects vary from person to person. And however carefully Mary Ann measured her doses of the poison, she would not always have been able to to be sure how strong the arsenic was that she was measuring out.

Soon after her arrival in Grace Street, Mary Ann was sleeping with the head of the household, James Robinson. This might be taken as evidence of Mary Ann's sexual appetite, but it could also be interpreted as a sign of James Robinson's powers as a seducer, or his loneliness after the death of his wife just a few months earlier. Since she must have known that she was pretty fertile, Mary Ann might have seduced her young master simply in order to get pregnant, and thus to lever him into what was for him a second marriage, and for her a third. In any case, by February 1866 Mary Ann was pregnant again – perhaps for the ninth time.

She may have felt that a speedy marriage to Robinson, and her position in his house, was now assured, but soon after she conceived, an obstacle was put in her way. She was called away to Seaham Colliery to nurse her mother, who was ill with hepatitis.

Hepatitis, which effects the liver, still counts as a serious infectious disease today, but most people make a full recovery after a few weeks, and don't even need any special medical treatment. Mary Ann would have found her mother, a woman in her mid-fifties, looking rather yellow in the face and giving off a peculiar odour. The urine in her chamber-pot would also have been brown and strange-smelling, and her stools would probably have been unusually pale.

If Mary Ann took the trouble to wash her mother, she would have noticed that the yellow colour of her skin came off, only to be replaced during natural perspiration. Close up, her daughter would have noticed that the whites of Margaret Stott's eyes were also yellow.

Although the disease she was suffering from is not usually fatal, Margaret Stott died just a few weeks after her daughter came to care for her. Hepatitis patients are generally advised to take plenty of fluids, and it may be that the fluids Mary Ann fed to her mother were tainted with arsenic. This would have amounted to a disastrous double whammy for Margaret's liver, since arsenic is known to have some particularly nasty effects on that organ. A Chinese study published in the year 2000 showed that residents of the city of Guizhou suffered from all sorts of liver problems because of long-term exposure to arsenic in their drinking-water.

The arsenic/hepatitis link was also a feature of a poisoning case in the 1970s. The first victim of Audrey Marie Hilley, an American arsenic poisoner, was thought to have died of hepatitis. The victim was Audrey's husband Frank, who passed away in May 1975. The diagnosis was only called into question in 1979 when Audrey's daughter Carol fell ill and was found to have tell-tale white lines across her finger-nails and toe-nails. These lines, called Mees' lines or Aldrich-Mees' lines, are indicators of poisoning by a heavy metal. When Frank's body was exhumed, unusually high levels of arsenic were found. Margaret Stott's doctors would not have understood the significance of any lines they found on her nails, as this symptom was not described until 1901. Audrey Hilley's husband and daughter were both heavily insured.

If the doctors had failed to recognise liver cancer, which shares some symptoms with hepatitis, then Margaret's death may not have been due to poison at all, although exposure to arsenic has been linked in some medical studies to a form of liver cancer.

With the death of her mother, Mary Ann was now responsible for Isabella Mowbray, the child she had left with Margaret, who was now eight years old. Isabella's step-grandfather, George Stott, was evidently not interested in the child. Mary Ann took her back to James Robinson's house at Pallion, where a number of suspicious deaths now ensued at a rapid pace.

Two of Robinson's children, his six-year old son James and his daughter Elizabeth, eight, as well as Mary Ann's daughter Isabella, all died just a few days apart in April 1867. This left Robinson with only two children – William, ten, and Mary Jane, three. James had died of 'continued fever' and the girls from 'gastric fever'. 'Gastric fever' is practically synonymous with typhoid, the symptoms of which can easily be reproduced by the use of arsenic.

The deaths of three children, in rapid succession and in one household, would be the cause for much concern, suspicion and a major investigation today, but in 1867 such tragedies were not unusual. Victorian medicine could do little against diseases like typhoid and cholera, and even the most privileged members of society could not escape them. In 1861 Queen Victoria's beloved husband Prince Albert died of typhoid, and in the year before Death beat his wings over James Robinson's house, a cholera epidemic had taken away some six thousand Britons.

Mary Ann gained little financial advantage from the death of her own daughter, and the beneficiary of any insurance or burial-club payouts for the Robinson children would of course have been their father. If Mary Ann did indeed kill the two Robinson children, then she would have reduced the amount of work she had to do around the house, and perhaps increased the time she could spend with their father, by whom she was already pregnant. As his children slipped through his hands, Robinson may have turned to Mary Ann for comfort: with the death of Isabella Mowbray and Margaret Stott, Mary Ann could now pose as a grieving mother, and she and James could comfort each other in their time of mourning.

By the beginning of August 1867 Mary Ann would have looked pregnant, even in the modest female clothing of the period. On the eleventh, she married James Robinson in Bishopwearmouth church. In memory, perhaps, of the mother and daughter Mary Ann had just lost, the daughter Mary Ann gave birth to in late November 1867 was baptised Margaret Isabella Robinson. She didn't live beyond the February of the next year, having died of convulsions before a doctor could diagnose the problem. In June of the next year, 1869, Mary Ann gave birth to a son, George Robinson.

GOODBYE TO PALLION

James Robinson's house was now home to little George, his two surviving children by his first wife, James himself and his housekeeper-turned-bride. There seemed to be no reason why Mary Ann's third marriage should not have continued happily, as long as her new husband did not suspect that she had killed three children under his roof. The marriage broke down, however, when Robinson found out, not about Mary Ann's murders, but about her dishonest ways with his money.

As housekeeper-turned-wife, Mary Ann had control of the purse-strings of the little family in Grace Street, Pallion. The purse was fairly large, as her new husband had got into the laudable habit of saving money with a local building society. In those days before ATM machines, online banking and electronic money, the savings system was based around old-fashioned pass-books or savings-books. When the building society member withdrew money or paid money in, the transaction was recorded in longhand in the savings-book, and a running total of the account would also be recorded. Matching information would also be recorded at the building society, perhaps in a large, leather-bound ledger with page after page of meticulously hand-ruled columns and copperplate entries.

If there was a discrepancy between the sums recorded in the member's savings-book and the society's ledger, then there was a problem. This, as well as blots and errors in the ledger, was the kind of possibility that was likely to keep a building society clerk awake at night.

Sometime in 1869 James Robinson was told that his new wife had been doctoring the entries in his savings-books to make it appear that Robinson had more money than he actually had. One can imagine her up late at night when everyone else was asleep, adding zeros to numbers and turning threes into eights, by the yellow light of an oil-lamp.

Robinson couldn't at first believe that Mary Ann would attempt such a clumsy fraud, but when he looked into the matter he found that not only had she doctored the savings-books; she had also withdrawn fifty pounds from his bank and borrowed sixty pounds in his name, without even telling him. Fifty pounds in 1869 would be worth well over two thousand today. Digging deeper, James also discovered that Mary Ann had been pawning items from his house, and had even pledged all his clothes as security for a loan. Mary Ann had been found out – but not for murder.

There is no evidence to suggest what Mary Ann was doing with all this money. She may have opened a secret savings account of her own, to act as an emergency reserve to draw on if she hit hard times again. She may have been giving money as gifts to a lover: she may even have kept bank-notes sewn into her clothes as an emergency fund. She certainly didn't spend the money on drink or gambling.

The way that she swindled her husband tends to indicate that, despite their cohabiting, the grief they shared, their love-making and the children they now had together, Mary Ann had not thrown in her lot with this man, psychologically. She may even have seen him as an enemy; someone likely to discover her dark secret; or as a mere 'mark' - someone to deceive. It may be that she did not consider herself worthy of her new family – as indeed she was not, if we are to believe that she was the poisoner she is supposed to have been. Her attempt to defraud the building society suggests a lack of intelligence or imagination on Mary Ann's part – surely she must have known that the bank had its own record of her transactions?

Married couples tend to argue most fiercely about money, and the almighty row that must have blown up over Mary Ann's frauds meant that the family split in two and Mary Ann left Pallion, with George, her little son by James Robinson. Why she should have taken George when she was evidently not too fond of children is a mystery. Perhaps she had developed a special attachment to the little boy, or perhaps she thought she could use him as a bargaining-chip in future negotiations with his father. She certainly returned to

Pallion in search of a reconciliation, but she found the locks changed and the house boarded up: Robinson had moved away.

It was at this point in her life that Mary Ann acquired an important new ally, in the shape of one of the leading men of Victorian Sunderland, Edward Backhouse. Through the help of Maling, a doctor she had worked with at the Sunderland Infirmary, Mary Ann gained a position on the staff of Ashburne, Backhouse's fine house, and also a position as chief laundress at a place called Smyrna House in Sunderland, which Backhouse had helped to set up. It is not clear whether Mary Ann worked first at Ashburne or at Smyrna House.

The position of laundress at Smyrna House had been advertised in a Quaker newspaper called *The British Friend* in July 1868. If the post had been filled at that time, then it must have become vacant again by the time Mary Ann filled it a year or so later. The advertisement describes Smyrna House as a 'female home and refuge', and refers to the community there as 'the family'; it also mentions 'a liberal salary'. What Smyrna House actually was was a home for 'fallen women', a type of place also known at the time as a penitentiary.

The idea of such places as Smyrna House was to give women who had been cast out of society, usually because of some behaviour that went against the Puritanical grain of Victorian respectability, a chance to 'reform' and perhaps become employable. The occupants of such places had sometimes worked as prostitutes – others had borne a child out of wedlock or been deserted by their husbands because of their excessive drinking, or their interest in other men.

'Fallen women' were victims of the Victorian double-standard whereby men could escape the consequences of, for instance, sexual promiscuity, while promiscuous women were left occupying an unenviable position under a black cloud of disapproval. The gravity that caused these women to fall seemed to be particularly strong in Sunderland: when a county penitentiary was set up in Durham City in Victorian times, a large proportion of the inmates were Sunderland women.

Edward Backhouse would have been in his early sixties when he first employed Mary Ann Robinson. He was a member of the Backhouse Quaker banking family, which also had interests in local collieries. Though he was a partner in the family business concerns, Edward and his wife Katharine devoted themselves to charitable activities – indeed it is estimated that they spent over ten thousand pounds a year on charity (worth over half a million today).

The fact that Mary Ann supervised a laundry in a home for fallen women does not, of course, mean that she was regarded as a fallen woman herself, although if the Backhouses had known about her sexual and financial indiscretions they might have been tempted to put her in that category. The 1868 job advert specifically appeals for 'a right-minded woman', which suggests that Mary Ann was able to keep up an appearance of respectability, and to conceal her murky past.

Mary Ann had of course taken baby George with her when she left Robinson. This baby she left with a Sunderland friend at the end of 1869, saying that she was just popping out to post a letter. She never came back, and little George Robinson was returned to his father in the new year.

FREDERICK COTTON

Working for the Backhouses, with her baby disposed of, Mary Ann had the means to make a new life for herself as an independent woman. The lure of marriage proved an irresistible temptation, however – Mary Ann was even prepared to commit bigamy to live as somebody's wife again.

The new man at whom Mary Ann now set her cap was Frederick Cotton, the brother of her old friend, Margaret Cotton. Like James Robinson, Frederick Cotton had recently been made a widower; and he had also lost one of his four children. Both of these deaths happened in the winter of 1868: in January 1870 he lost another child to typhus.

Frederick Cotton was a coal-miner by profession and lived in the Northumberland mining village of North Walbottle, to the north-west of Newcastle. He was a hewer at the Coronation pit which, like the nearby Blucher pit, had been sunk in 1800. The Coronation was named for the coronation of William IV – the name of the Blucher commemorated the Russian Field Marshall Blucher, one of the heroes of the Battle of Waterloo. A hewer was a miner who actually hacked the coal from the coal-face, a tough job often performed in cramped, hot and dangerous conditions.

Frederick Cotton's sister Margaret had given up her job in service and moved in with him to help run the household, but it was clear that Frederick was in need of a new wife. When Margaret introduced him to Mary Ann, the die was cast. She became pregnant in the spring of 1870, and, probably to avoid scandal, she went away to Spennymoor in her home county of Durham. There she worked in the household of a German physician, and may have stolen his watch, as well as some money and valuables. The theft was, however, blamed on the doctor's groom, who was dismissed.

In September 1870 Frederick and the by now no doubt visibly pregnant Mary Ann married at St Andrew's Church, Newcastle. The marriage was bigamous, as James Robinson, Mary Ann's 'previous' husband, was still alive. Mary Ann had had a clandestine marriage in Newcastle before, of course, when she married her first husband, William Mowbray, in 1852. That time, it was a register office wedding – this time, she married in the oldest church in Newcastle, parts of which date from the twelfth century.

It is unlikely that Frederick and Mary Ann thought much about the church's long and turbulent history on their wedding day in 1870. For them, this city-centre church offered the anonymity of Newcastle, a large settlement where they were unlikely to bump into anyone they knew. The witnesses were two acquaintances from North Walbottle: no old friends or family were present, as far as we know. Both bride and groom claimed to be residents of the Newcastle parish of St Andrew's (which they weren't) and Mary Ann gave her married surname by her first husband – Mowbray.

In Victorian times, divorce was out of the question for people of Mary Ann's status and income. Unmarried cohabitation (still called 'living in sin' by some people) was frowned on; and the result was that an awful lot of people risked bigamy. In a 2008 book called *Living in sin*, Ginger Frost implies that between 1857 and 1904 there may have been as many as five hundred bigamous weddings a year in England and Wales. Frost remarks that the sentences meted out to the hundred or so bigamists who were caught and tried every year were surprisingly lenient, many offenders spending less than a month in prison.

It is possible that Frederick Cotton never knew that his second marriage was illegal, and he may not even have known that Mary Ann had married a James Robinson at all. He may have known nothing of her second husband, George Ward, and believed she had been a widow since William Mowbray died of typhus in 1865. Mary Ann may have been very economical with the truth about her past life, both with Frederick and his sister, her friend Margaret Cotton. Margaret died shortly after Mary Ann first moved in with the Cottons, of pleuropneumonia, a type of lung infection the symptoms of which couldn't easily have been simulated by arsenic poisoning. Mary Ann did benefit indirectly from the death of her friend, however: her new husband Frederick would have inherited the savings of sixty pounds that Margaret had amassed (worth nearly three thousand pounds today).

By moving in with Frederick at North Walbottle Mary Ann was moving out of the big city of Sunderland, where coal-mining was by no means the only form of adult male employment, and into a village like those in which she had spent so much of her early life, where coal was practically the only reason for the existence of the settlement at all. During its decades of work, over twenty million tons of coal were extracted from the North Walbottle pit. It was closed in 1968, for a reason that Frederick and Mary Ann would no doubt have found quite fantastic – it was feared that the workings would weaken the runways at Newcastle Airport.

A month or so after their bigamous marriage, Mary Ann persuaded Frederick to insure the lives of his two remaining children, Frederick and Charles, who were eight and four years old. Frederick Cotton senior already had life insurance.

Mary Ann's child by Frederick Cotton, christened Robert Robson Cotton, was born five months after their bigamous marriage. Soon the Cottons, 'husband' and 'wife' and three boys, moved out of North Walbottle and ended up at West Auckland, the Durham mining village that is forever associated with the name of Mary Ann Cotton, though she lived there only briefly. The doomed family would have moved in early April, when the mining bond whereby Frederick Cotton was tied to employment at the Coronation colliery in North Walbottle would have expired. It is likely that many other families were moving at this time, since it was effectively a breach of contract for miners to change employment while the annual bond was in force.

It may be that Frederick and Mary Ann thought there were better opportunities awaiting them at West Auckland, but they may have had other reasons for moving. Everybody at North Walbottle would have known that Mary Ann had conceived her latest child out of wedlock, and local disapproval may have made life difficult for her in the village. It is also possible that news of the existence of her 'previous' husband James Robinson had somehow reached Northumberland, and that whispers were spreading; about bigamy and about a large number of deaths surrounding Frederick Cotton's new bedfellow.

Whatever Frederick and the children thought about the move, Mary Ann, as we shall see, may have had her own secret reason for moving to West Auckland.

WEST AUCKLAND

County Durham was not included in the Domesday Book, as it was ruled almost as a separate kingdom within England. In this anomalous county, the Bishop of Durham reigned as a Prince Bishop. The Durham equivalent to the Domesday Book is the Boldon Book, a survey commissioned by Bishop Hugh du Puiset in 1183. West Auckland features in the Boldon Book, where we are told that eighteen 'villans' or peasants lived there. H. Conyers Surtees tells us, in a 1924 book about the area, that the village 'is three and a half miles south-west from Bishop Auckland, is of considerable size, and pleasantly situated on the [River] Gaunless, which is here spanned by a stone bridge'.

A less attractive picture of the village was given by a Mr Stobart in 1853, at the sessions held in July of that year. Stobart said the drainage was so bad that West Auckland was frequently under water. He also said that it was one of the filthiest places in England, and that 'the only thing to improve it would be a good flood or fire'. In 1924, when Surtees wrote his book, West Auckland Colliery was still operating, as was Norless Colliery to the north-west. There were also stone and slate quarries to the north.

At West Auckland, the Cottons lived on Johnson Terrace, now called Darlington Road. Mary Ann's secret reason for moving to West Auckland was right there in another house in the same street – her red-headed lover Joseph Nattrass, now a widower, lived in lodgings in Johnson Terrace.

Frederick Cotton found work, as a hewer again, at West Auckland Colliery, but his employment there didn't last long. He was taken ill at work and died in September 1871 of typhoid and hepatitis. Since he was well-insured, and Mary Ann's lover lived in the same street, this death looks very suspicious. As we know, the symptoms of arsenic poisoning are similar to those of typhoid, and as we saw in connection with the death of Mary Ann's mother, there can also be a link between liver disease and arsenic.

At this point in her story, Mary Ann's life became even more complicated than it had been before. After a pause of three months, her old lover Joseph Nattrass moved into the house in Johnson Terrace as a lodger. It soon became known that he was to marry Mary Ann. The stage was, therefore, set for Mary Ann to start a family again with a new husband, plus two of Frederick Cotton's children from his first marriage, and her own child by Frederick. This is not, however, what happened at all.

Despite her responsibilities at home, and the easy access she now had to Joseph Nattrass, Mary Ann advertised her services as a nurse and found a job in the house of a Mr Quick-Manning, who lived at Brookfield Cottage, a rather nice house, also in Johnson Terrace. Quick-Manning was a bachelor who was recovering from small-pox, a disease which has now been all but eradicated. It used to kill around thirty percent of its victims, which means that Quick-Manning was fairly lucky to have survived it. He may have had the less serious version of the disease, known as variola minor, which rarely causes death.

Following the pattern that she had established with James Robinson and Frederick Cotton, Mary Ann was soon setting her cap at Quick-Manning, who worked as the excise officer at a local brewery. The obvious barriers to any closer relationship with Quick-Manning, Joseph Nattrass and the three children at home, were soon being eliminated to clear Mary Ann's progress to a better house in the same street.

Within twenty-two days, from March the tenth to April the first 1892, Nattrass, Frederick Cotton junior and Robert, Mary Ann's child by Frederick Cotton senior, were all dead. Nattrass was registered as having died of typhoid fever, Frederick (aged ten) of gastric fever, and little Robert from convulsions caused by teething. Needless to say, arsenic could have brought on symptoms that doctors at the time could have mistaken for these conditions. Frederick and Robert both had life insurance. Nattrass had none, but he left his savings of ten pounds and fifteen shillings to Mary Ann. This sum would be worth around five hundred pounds today.

Although he had managed to fight off small pox, it seems that Quick-Manning the excise officer could not fight off Mary Ann. As a woman who probably had far more experience of sex that he had, she would have known how to brush aside all his Victorian middle-class scruples. Even if he had been lucky enough to gain some sexual experience as a bachelor, few Victorian women would have taken the lead in such matters as, by this time, Mary Ann was probably doing. Shortly after the death of her lover Joseph Nattrass, Mary Ann was pregnant by Quick-Manning.

The last surviving child left with Mary Ann was seven year old Charles Edward Cotton. If we accept that Mary Ann poisoned Nattrass, Frederick and Robert, then we must ask ourselves why Charles Edward, who was only her step-child, was spared. She certainly didn't like the boy, and according to the neighbours she beat him and starved him, left him alone in the house, sometimes for days on end, and locked him out in all weathers. It is possible that Mary Ann kept the boy alive, albeit grudgingly, because with the seven year-old in the house, she was in receipt of parish relief – the Victorian equivalent of social security benefit.

By this time, Mary Ann had moved to Front Street in West Auckland. Here, on July the sixth 1872, Mary Ann Cotton, serial killer and now also cruel stepmother to a living child, met her nemesis.

Nemesis came in the shape of Thomas Riley, overseer of local parish relief, who called on Mary Ann to ask her to act as a nurse for another small pox victim. She complained that she couldn't earn money in that way because she had to look after little Charles Edward. She had tried to palm him off on her late husband's relatives, but they didn't want him. She now suggested that Riley take him into the workhouse, but Riley said he couldn't unless Mary Ann came too. Mary Ann refused to go to the workhouse, but remarked that, like the rest of the Cotton family, Charles Edward was weak and likely to die soon.

When Riley told Mary Ann that he couldn't take Charles Edward to the workhouse, he was being a little economical with the truth. If she had abandoned him and disowned him, he would have had to take Charles Edward, because he would have had nowhere else to go. The workhouse in question would have been the one on Cockton Hill in the nearby town of Bishop Auckland, which opened in 1855 and was governed by the Auckland Poor Law Union.

Workhouses were a harsh and old-fashioned attempt at a solution to the problem of poverty – the first English workhouses began to operate in the seventeenth century, but they were not officially abolished until 1930. The idea was that people too old or ill to support themselves would be housed in these institutions. To guard against the dangers of idleness, inmates were given hard and sometimes pointless work to do – hence the 'work' part of the word 'workhouse'.

Admission to a workhouse was an admission of poverty, incapacity and failure of family support – people of Mary Ann Cotton's generation feared such places, sometimes more than they feared death itself. This fear, and the stigma that attached to workhouse inmates and ex-inmates, continued among the generation born around the turn of the nineteenth and twentieth centuries. Some members of this generation even dreaded buildings that had once been workhouses, and had been converted into retirement homes or hospitals.

It seems that poverty was relieved in West Auckland by a combination of 'outdoor relief' – that is, cash paid to hard-up people who remained in their homes, and 'indoor relief' for those forced to enter the workhouse. As an unemployed mother and widow, Mary Ann was in receipt of outdoor relief from the organisation Riley represented. It seems that, to get people like Mary Ann off relief, Riley acted as a kind of one-man employment bureau, which is how he was able to offer her a job as a nurse.

During her conversation with Riley - perhaps the most fateful exchange of words in the whole of Mary Ann's short life - she got the idea that Riley was about to take her off parish relief, and leave her penniless. Riley later denied this, but whatever was said, or understood to have been said, the damage was done. Mary Ann's financial incentive for keeping Charles Edward alive was, at least in her own mind, removed.

There is no doubt that little Charles Edward Cotton would have fared better in Bishop Auckland's workhouse than he did at home with his step-mother. Six days after her conversation with Riley, Charles Edward was dead.

RILEY'S CAMPAIGN

Thomas Riley, who was around fifty years of age in 1872, was a local shop-keeper who sold groceries, and also some of the things we might expect to find in a pharmacy today. He was also a farmer – a combination of concerns that made him something of a wealthy local self-made man. His role as an overseer of local parish relief suggests that he was also a solid citizen and a pillar of the community.

He lived right across the village green from Mary Ann with his young wife, and three children from his previous marriage. It is possible that Riley himself or one of his employees actually sold Mary Ann the arsenic she used to kill four people in West Auckland. This came in the form of arsenical soft soap – a lethal Victorian version of modern washing-up liquid.

Charles Edward Cotton was treated during his last illness by a local physician called Kilburn, who may have been related to Thomas Riley. Riley suggested to Kilburn that there might be foul play in the case, and as a consequence Kilburn refused to issue a death certificate. This meant that Mary Ann could not claim Charles Edward's life insurance money from the Prudential insurance company – an amount that may have been worth as much as four hundred pounds in modern money.

Questions over Charles Edward's death, and the lack of a death-certificate, triggered an inquest overseen by a coroner. Coroners are a very ancient type of legal official under English law, dating from Norman times. Their role is to investigate doubtful or suspicious deaths and, where there is a question of foul play, the verdict of the coroner's inquest may sit alongside the outcome of any criminal trial. In this case, the inquest was held in the Rose and Crown public house, which was then right next door to Mary Ann's home. The inquest considered the findings of Dr Kilburn's autopsy of Charles

Edward Cotton. We can get some idea of how unlike a modern forensic autopsy this was when we learn that it was carried out on a table in Mary Ann's own kitchen. Charles Edward's body was probably laid out in a coffin in the house, awaiting burial, as was the custom of the time.

Kilburn found traces of a white powder in the child's digestive system, but he assumed that these were the remains of medicines that he himself had prescribed for the boy. The inquest returned a verdict of death by natural causes. At this point, Kilburn did not attempt a chemical analysis of any material from the body. He did, however, retain liquid from the stomach in a jar, and buried the stomach itself in his own garden.

Thomas Riley was not satisfied with the verdict of the inquest, and he seems to have pressurised Kilburn into taking a closer look at the remains of Charles Edward that he still had in his possession. Although he was an ordinary family doctor, or general practitioner, with no specialist training in forensic science, Kilburn nevertheless rigged up an apparatus to apply Reinsch's test for poisonous metals. This test was introduced by the German chemist Hugo Reinsch some thirty years before Charles Edward's death.

The test involves heating suspect materials mixed with hydrochloric acid. During the test, a piece of copper foil is added to the mixture. If the copper becomes coated with a silvery substance, then mercury, a poisonous metal, is indicated. If the copper goes dark, then the experimenter has probably found arsenic, antimony or one of a range of other poisonous heavy metals.

The Reinsch test is unreliable, not just because it can only indicate one of a range of heavy metals: false positives can happen if the chemist uses impure acid or copper. Arsenic can be a by-product of the smelting of copper, so it is not surprising that arsenic in the copper itself sometimes gave a false positive, in the early days of the test. The Reinsch test is still used by toxicologists today, but it is usually followed up with more modern tests such as absorption or emission spectroscopy, or X-ray diffraction.

Durham law courts (Miranda Brown)

Victorian Sunderland (DCC)

St Andrew's church, Newcastle, where Mary Ann
was 'married' to Frederick Cotton (MB)

Sign of the Half Moon pub in Durham, where
Mary Ann's jury took their meals (MB)

William Calcraft (WM)

The photograph (WM)

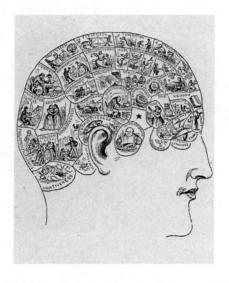

Phrenological map of the human head (WM)

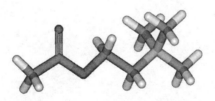

Molecule for acetylcholene,
a brain chemical that can change behaviour (WM)

Florence Maybrick and her husband James (WM)

Marie Brinvilliers being put to the ordinary question (WM)

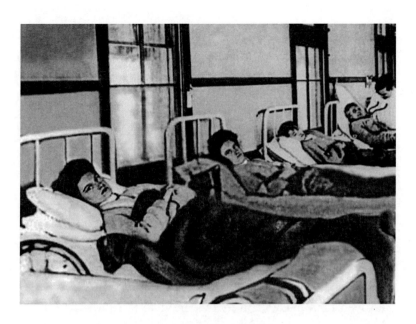

Typhoid Mary (WM)

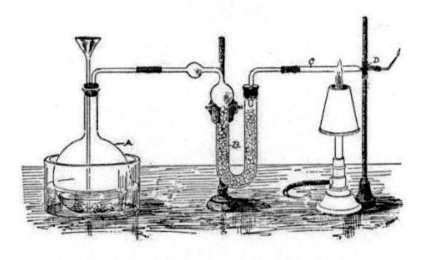

Marsh test for arsenic (WM)

ALFRED D. PURSE,

(FORMERLY SENIOR ASSISTANT TO HER MAJESTY'S CHYMIST)

DISPENSING CHYMIST,

15 Salem Street, Sunderland.

Physicians' Prescriptions accurately prepared with genuine Drugs and Chemicals at moderate charges.

Advert for a Sunderland chemist in Victorian times (DCC)

Unidentified Victorian portrait photographer (WM)

MRS GREEN

It would seem that poison and poisoning are ever-present in human history, even where that history shades into myth and legend. Poisons, including the herbal poison hemlock, are mentioned in the Bible, and in the character of Medea we have something like an archetypal female poisoner from Greek mythology.

Medea used an unspecified poison to murder her husband Jason's child by another woman, and also the two children she had by him. In the play by the Greek playwright Euripides, she explains that as a woman wanting to commit murder, poison is a natural choice for her. In the character of Medea we have the combination of a type of witch or enchantress with a poisoner. This link may have existed in the ancient Greek mind because for them medicine, science and magic were more closely connected than they are for modern people in the West. Medea is also like Mary Ann Cotton in that, having poisoned Jason's children, she goes on to marry another man, whose child she also tries to poison.

Circe, who appears in Homer's *Odyssey*, is another enchantress who uses a potion to turn Odysseus' companions into pigs. Like Mary Ann Cotton, she has considerable feminine charms, which she uses to detain Odysseus on her island.

If it is true that she used arsenic to poison her victims, Mary Ann was employing a substance that has existed alongside the human race since prehistoric times. Ötzi, the frozen prehistoric man found in the Ötztal Alps in Austria in 1991, was found to be quite saturated with arsenic. It is thought that the poison had got into his five-thousand year-old body because he had been smelting copper – that is to say, extracting copper from one of its ores. Arsenic appears as an impurity in many metal ores and, as we have seen, can persist in impure samples of the final product. If Ötzi, who was carrying a copper axe when he died, had been smelting that metal using the technology of his time, then he could easily have taken in a lot of arsenic by this means.

Two compounds containing arsenic – the red realgar and yellow orpiment – were popular cosmetics in ancient times, and a container with orpiment inside it was found in the tomb of Tutankhamen, who died over fifteen hundred years ago. Mithridates VI, a king of Pontus in Anatolia who died in 63 BC, is said to have taken minute quantities of various poisons, including arsenic, so that he would be immune to any poisons his enemies might manage to slip into his food or drink.

In the eighth century AD a tasteless white compound of arsenic was created by an Arabic alchemist called Jabir ibn Hayyan. This so-called arsenious acid was a godsend to would-be poisoners, and was employed by the powerful Borgia family in Renaissance Italy; although the reputation Lucrezia Borgia acquired as a poisoning adept is probably undeserved.

Arsenic works by switching off cells in the body, much as a thrifty house-keeper will extinguish all the lights in a house before going to bed. The body recognises arsenic as an irritant, and tries to purge it through vomiting and diarrhoea. Sometimes this reaction can save the patient, but if too much arsenic is given too quickly, or if it is given in small doses over a long period, it will embed itself in the body and bring the victim to the grave. Symptoms of acute arsenic poisoning include headache, confusion, convulsions, drowsiness, paralysis, blood in the urine, hair-loss, changes in the appearance of the skin, and even night-blindness.

As a murder weapon, arsenic is particularly nasty as it can cause severe stomach-pain. The pain aspect is one reason why arsenic is not popular as a method of suicide, although in Gustave Flaubert's 1856 French novel *Madame Bovary* the eponymous heroine employs it, to horrific effect:

Her chest soon began panting rapidly; the whole of her tongue protruded from her mouth; her eyes, as they rolled, grew paler, like the two globes of a lamp that is going out, so that one might have thought her already dead but for the fearful labouring of her ribs, shaken by violent breathing, as if the soul were struggling to free itself.

Also in France, but in the seventeenth century, lived a woman who was in many ways similar to Mary Ann Cotton, although her background and the milieu in which she lived were quite different. Like Mary Ann, Marie Madeleine de Brinvilliers was strikingly attractive: in the same way that Mary Ann stood out in the north of England because of her dark good looks, the blonde, blue-eyed Marquise was unusual among French women.

Marie Madeleine's childhood was a strange combination of neglect (from her parents) and too much attention (from the numerous servants employed at their grand house in Paris). The little blonde girl grew up spoiled and manipulative, able to twist men, including her father, round her little finger. As a married woman she had many lovers, including the hapless tutor of her children, and the Chevalier Gaudin de Sainte Croix, a handsome aristocrat who was also an amateur chemist.

Numerous pregnancies were the natural result of Marie Madeleine's amorous adventures, but the children were not an encumbrance to her because she only had to see them when she wanted to: at other times they were looked after by wet-nurses, servants and tutors.

Like many other members of the French aristocracy at the time, Marie Madeleine was unable to live within her means, and sometimes she couldn't leave her house because of the creditors who clamoured outside. Together with the Chevalier, she hatched a plan to kill her own father, so as to inherit at least part of his wealth.

Before the pair could attempt the proposed murder, Marie Madeleine tested the poisons formulated by the Chevalier on patients at the Hotel de Dieu, a struggling hospital right next to Paris's famous Notre Dame Cathedral. At the Hotel, Marie Madeleine acted as a kind of volunteer visitor or assistant nurse: nursing was of course a profession followed at times by Mary Ann Cotton.

Her poisons now thoroughly tested, Marie Madeleine set about poisoning her father, while pretending to help nurse him through a serious illness. Her goal was quickly achieved, and despite an autopsy, poison was not suspected – or at least, no evidence for its use was found. This act of killing a parent (her mother was already dead from natural causes) is another thing that makes Mary Ann and Marie Madeleine sisters in poison.

Marie Madeleine's extravagance was so great, that the inheritance she now shared with her two brothers and her sister made little impression on her debts. Soon she was conspiring with the Chevalier to kill her brothers. She persuaded these brothers, Antoine and André, to take on a servant called 'Gaston La Chausée'. This man was in fact a rascal called Jean Hamelin, whom the Chevalier had trained in the art of poison. He slowly poisoned the Brinvilliers brothers, and again the doctors were unable or unwilling to find evidence of murder. Again the money Marie Madeleine could now share with her surviving sibling – a nun – counted for little, and to make matters worse the Chevalier now sought to control Marie Madeleine by the use of blackmail.

The next natural target for the poisoning partnership would have been Marie Madeleine's husband, but like many rich and powerful people in France at the time, the Marquis de Brinvilliers feared poison and took elaborate precautions to avoid it. In any case, Marie Madeleine's collaborator in her deadly work, the Chevalier de Sainte Croix, died in his laboratory before the pair could try to poison him. It seems that the Chevalier had been trying to develop a poison gas that would be even less detectable in the bodies of victims than the liquids he had used previously. Evidently, his experiments had met with success, but not in the way he had anticipated.

The Chevalier had written out a confession of his crimes, which was burned straight away by the investigators, because such written confessions were supposed to be addressed to God, and were not for human eyes. The casket of poisons found by the Chevalier's body was, however, very incriminating. They were thoroughly examined, and tested on various unfortunate animals (including a turkey) but, with the primitive chemistry of the time, nothing could be made of them, though it was pretty clear to everyone that they were poisons.

La Chaussée, the servant the Chevalier had trained as a poisoner, was now captured by the authorities and, terrified of discovery, Marie Madeleine fled to London, then to Belgium where she found sanctuary in a nunnery. When the area came under French control, Marie Madeleine was finally captured and brought back to Paris. There she was subjected to a very lengthy trial with many witnesses, but the most damning witness against her was her own confession, which she had written out in the nunnery.

After much legal consideration, the court determined that Marie Madeleine's written confession could be used against her in court. Among other admissions, the document contained the revelation that Marie Madeleine had helped another woman to poison someone, and that she had committed incest with her brothers at a very young age.

Maître Nivelle, her defence counsel, argued that, after an upbringing lacking in moral instruction, Marie Madeleine had fallen under the spell of the wicked Chevalier de Sainte Croix and had acted as his puppet in the various evil deeds into which he had led her. Though delivered with apparent sincerity, Nivelle's defence counted for little in the face of such damning evidence as that presented by Briancourt, the tutor of Marie Madeleine's children, a lover to whom she had confessed everything.

Marie Madeleine de Brinvilliers was condemned to death and, as a matter of course it seems, she was put to the 'ordinary question', a form of torture which was surely unnecessary in her case since she had by now confessed everything to her new spiritual adviser, the Abbé Pirot. The ordinary question involved stretching the victim backwards over a low form, then forcing him or her to drink gallons of water poured down a leather funnel.

After her public execution at the Place de Greve in Paris, Marie Madeleine was immortalised in a book by the elder Alexandre Dumas, author of *The three musketeers* and *The Count of Monte Cristo*.

The differences between the cases of Marie Madeleine and Mary Ann Cotton are if anything more illuminating than the similarities. Mary Ann seems to have carried out all her crimes alone, without any connivance with other people. Marie Madeleine, by contrast, collaborated with her lover, the Chevalier, and his servant La

Chaussée. Unlike Mary Ann, she may not even have been able to obtain arsenic on her own, since such a grand lady was not expected to purchase items from pharmacists unattended in those days.

Marie Madeleine confessed her sins to the tutor Briancourt: Mary Ann, by contrast, never seems to have made a full confession of anything except her bigamous marriage to Frederick Cotton.

Mary Ann was able to operate in secret partly because she was entirely obscure – just another working-class housewife in the north of England. Marie Madeleine, by contrast, became notorious for her scandalous behaviour shortly after her marriage: even the manner of her first meeting with her future husband became hot gossip (some said she had met him while walking alone in a disreputable Paris street: others said they had met in a brothel, where she had gone to get some pre-marital sexual experience).

The West Auckland poisoner evaded detection by regularly moving around within the then generous confines of County Durham, and Northumberland. Marie Madeleine spent practically her whole life in her father's large house in Paris – her father was reduced to living in just a handful of rooms after Marie Madeleine, her husband and her lovers took over the rest of the house.

The trial of Marie Madeleine de Brinvilliers was much more thorough than the scant three days it took to condemn Mary Ann to the rope. Marie's trial began on the twenty-ninth of April 1676, and ended on the sixteenth of July. During these months, there were twenty-two hearings, and the testimony of the tutor Briancourt alone lasted for thirteen hours.

Whereas the majority of Mary Ann's victims may have been children, La Brinvilliers may not have killed a single child, though we are told that she once gave a non-lethal dose of arsenic to one of her daughters, out of boredom. It would not have made sense for the Frenchwoman to poison children at the Hotel de Dieu, since she was testing poisons there before using them on adults – surely she would have realised that children would not make a good test-bed for poisons destined to be used on her father and her grown-up brothers.

Few of the people Mary Ann Cotton may have killed were subjected to autopsies after death, but Marie Madeleine's victims certainly were – they were after all important people, and they lived at a time when public hysteria about poisoning was maintained at a high level.

It is also likely that the doctors who attended Marie Madeleine's brothers and father would have been paid handsomely for their efforts at the autopsy table – by contrast there was precious little money available to pay for such services in Mary Ann's day, especially for poor people. The doctors who attended the upper echelons of French society in Marie Madeleine's time may have been less inclined to attribute the deaths of their wealthier clients to typhoid, and thus dismiss the need for further investigation – typhoid was a disease more likely to strike the poor.

The fact that no poison was found during these autopsies speaks to the primitive state of chemistry at the time: it was not until 1836 that the Marsh test for arsenic was developed – a test that was improved on by the introduction of the Reinsch test in 1841.

The doctors who examined the bodies of Marie Madeleine's victims did notice red and inflamed stomachs in some cases; and reddening of the sufferers' faces was noted as they lay dying. Nobody seems to have noted any tell-tale white granules of arsenic adhering to the stomach wall: this may have been because Marie Madeleine, the Chevalier and La Chausée preferred to poison slowly so that all the poison would be absorbed and none could be found in the stomach after death.

The Chevalier and his lover may have used a variety of poisons, which would explain Marie Madeleine's extensive 'testing' at the hospital by Notre Dame. The typhoid-like symptoms suffered by some of their victims would, however, seem to indicate that they used arsenic some of the time: by contrast it is likely that Mary Ann Cotton only ever used arsenic for poisoning.

Both Mary Ann Cotton and Marie Madeleine de Brinvilliers had numerous sexual partners, something that gives a certain erotic tinge to their stories. Unlike Mary Ann Cotton, Marie Madeleine had only one husband, but like many women of her class and situation at the time, she took lovers. This was accepted by Parisian high society, but only if the people involved were discreet. Marie Madeleine seemed not to know the meaning of discretion, and she and the Chevalier even went to a masked ball together and *took off their masks*.

Mary Ann Cotton seems to have had sex with all of her husbands before marriage, to have had at least one extra-marital affair, and to have married Frederick Cotton bigamously. It can be argued that her pre-marital affairs with all of her husbands were calculated to ensnare them into marriage by making them fathers, but her involvement with the red-headed miner Joseph Nattrass happened at a time when she was already married to her first husband, Mowbray. Nattrass must have known this, even if Mary Ann didn't know that Joseph was a married man.

Since Mary Ann probably didn't murder her first husband to marry Nattrass (which would have been impossible with his wife still alive) we must conclude that Mary Ann did not just use sex as a tool to manipulate men – she also seems to have regarded it as a hobby. There is also a suggestion that her second husband, the sickly George Ward, may have been unable to keep up with Mary Ann sexually, and had to be 'put away' for this reason.

Since Marie Madeleine and Mary Ann Cotton were both supposed to be strikingly good-looking, then it may not have been difficult for either of them to seduce men. Mary Ann might have had more trouble in this area than Marie Madeleine, since the aristocracy of seventeenth-century France were expected to be promiscuous, as long as they obeyed certain unwritten rules. Mary Ann's world was dominated by non-conformist ideas of purity and respectability, and it is possible that the girl from Low Moorsley had to work hard to get some of her men into bed.

It is interesting to note that Mary Ann Cotton and Marie Madeleine de Brinvilliers both had rather pious mothers. In the case of Marie Madeleine's mother, her piety showed itself in her work for worthy charities: Mrs Robson's Christianity may have manifested itself in a certain cold aloofness and puritanism. This may explain why Mary Ann's mother only ever had three children, though she was married for a long time, and to two different men. Her coldness may have left Mary Ann feeling unloved, and may have been the reason why she married her first husband in secret, and also why the newlywed

Mowbrays felt obliged to move away from the north-east when Mary Ann's first pregnancy began to show.

Nearly a century and a half after Marie Madeleine was beheaded by a swordsman on the Place de Greve in Paris (and not before many more French people had lost their heads) Napoleon Bonaparte died on the South Atlantic island of Saint Helena. An examination of the imperial body revealed the presence of arsenic, but it is not known whether the fallen emperor had been deliberately poisoned, had been taking preventative quantities like Mithridates, or had been inadvertently poisoned by his arsenic-coloured wallpaper.

In an alarming book called *Arsenic century: How Victorian Britain was poisoned at home, work and play*, the American medical historian James C. Whorton gives a horribly detailed picture of the ubiquity of arsenic in nineteenth-century England – the England of Mary Ann Cotton.

To give some idea of how the Victorians lived with arsenic every day of their lives we need to invent a typical Victorian lady of the middle-classes. We will call her Mrs Green.

Mrs Green wakes every morning to the sound of her children playing on the floorboards of the nursery, just above the bedroom she shares with her husband, a successful brewer who is some years her senior. The little Greens love to play with their wooden toys, painted in arsenical paint, and with their soft toys made with real fur, dusted with an arsenic compound to stop it rotting. The book-case in the nursery contains several books with covers dyed with arsenical colours.

In keeping with tradition, the nursery is rather spartan, with no wallpaper or carpets. By contrast, the adult Greens' bedroom has arsenical wallpaper in a rich, vivid green. There are also matching curtains and bed-hangings dyed with arsenical compounds. The bedroom carpet has very little arsenic in it, but the sheep who surrendered the wool had been dipped in an arsenic-rich sheep-dip.

Before breakfast, Mr Green secretly takes some pills containing arsenic, which he believes will increase his sexual potency and help him keep up with the demands of his pale young wife. Mrs Green secretly takes an arsenical medicine to preserve her fashionable pallor. She also applies an arsenical liquid to her face to prevent pimples.

Later, as the Greens eat their evening meal, the poorer people of the town are enthusiastically consuming beer produced by Green's brewery. The beer is made using glucose as a substitute for malt – glucose tainted with arsenic.

Whorton's book makes it clear that arsenic in different amounts, taken in different ways, had a variety of effects on different people, and that some people – for instance some of those exposed to heavy and repeated doses in their daily work – remained unaffected by the poison. Even if our fictitious Green husband and wife were naturally somewhat immune to the deadly effects of arsenic, their habit of ingesting the poison as a medication still posed a hidden risk. If, for instance, Mr Green had died of typhoid, the symptoms of which are similar to the symptoms of arsenical poisoning, an autopsy might have revealed arsenic throughout his system, as well as undigested fragments of the poison in his stomach. If the police had been unable to find evidence of Green's having taken arsenic willingly, then suspicion may have fallen upon his young wife, who might have been charged with his murder.

Something similar happened to Florence Maybrick, an American woman with a much older English husband, who was a dealer in cotton. When Maybrick died at their house in Liverpool in 1889, suspicion fell on Florence, who was known to have committed adultery with another man. She was at first sentenced to death for murder, but this sentence was later changed to life imprisonment. Eventually, she was released, in 1904: she died in 1941.

The initial trial of Florence Maybrick had not taken enough notice of the fact that her husband habitually dosed himself with arsenic and other poisons, and had been given arsenic, strychnine, henbane, morphia, prussic acid and other poisons by his doctors as he lay dying. Witnesses had seen Florence attempting to extract arsenic from fly-papers, but she claimed that this was intended for use on her own face, to clarify her complexion.

It was not unusual for defence counsel engaged by people accused of arsenic poisoning to claim that the supposed victims had ingested the poison by accident, or had been taking it as a medicine. The latter claim was known as the Styrian defence, after the natives of Styria in southern Austria, who in the middle of the nineteenth century were found to be taking terrifyingly high doses of arsenic, supposedly with no ill effects. Indeed, some claimed that the Styrians thrived on this frightening regime.

There is a link between Florence Maybrick and Mary Ann Cotton – Charles Russell, the eminent lawyer who prosecuted Mary Ann also defended Florence. The bungling judge who presided at Florence's trial was, incidentally, uncle to the writer Virginia Woolf.

Seventeen Grains of Arsenic

On the morning after Dr Kilburn used Reinsch's test to decide that little Charles Edward Cotton had been murdered, his step-mother was arrested. Instinctively, it seems, she chose silence in the face of her accusers, rather as Dr Harold Shipman did nearly one hundred and thirty years later. Shipman, a family doctor who may have murdered over two hundred of his patients, is thought to have been the first English serial killer to break Mary Ann Cotton's grim record for numbers of victims killed.

Cotton's silence may have been a continuation of a habit that had preserved her from detection for many years. It is unlikely that she ever told anyone her secrets – a wise habit for a guilty person who doesn't want to be caught. In her case, she had to conceal not only her murders, but also her attempts to swindle her third husband James Robinson out of his money, and the bigamy she committed when she married Frederick Cotton. She would also have kept quiet about her extra-marital affairs, and her pregnancies out of wedlock.

A few days after the arrest of his step-mother, the body of Charles Edward Cotton was dug up, and arsenic was found in various organs. Tests on samples from the exhumed boy were carried out by Dr Thomas Scattergood, lecturer in forensic medicine and toxicology at the Leeds School of Medicine. Scattergood also examined samples from the exhumed bodies of Frederick Cotton junior and Robert Robson Cotton, and again found arsenic. Samples of earth from the graveyard had also been taken up and tested for arsenic, but none was found. This meant that Mary Ann's defence counsel could not claim that arsenic had seeped into the bodies after burial.

Scattergood, a Yorkshireman whose entire career seems to have taken place in Leeds, had been a general practitioner for a very short time before starting to teach at the Leeds School of Medicine. After the School merged with the Yorkshire College, Scattergood became Dean of the Faculty of Medicine in 1884, and held this position until his death in 1900. As we shall see, Scattergood's evidence as an expert witness in court proved devastating for Mary Ann. Her defence team, such as it was, had little or nothing with which to answer it.

The body of the boys' father could not be found. In his 1987 book on the Cotton case, Derek Hebden paints a lively picture of the search for Frederick senior in the graveyard at St Helen Auckland. Working in the wee small hours of a foggy October morning, a group of men dug up grave after grave, directed by Joe Drummond, the sexton. They resumed two days later, digging up another twelve graves, but still had no luck. Drummond declared that there had been a hundred and sixteen burials in his churchyard since the new year 'an aw dun know a tithe o' em'. The graves were said to be 'as thick and close as furrows in a lea field'.

The body of Joseph Nattrass had been recovered a month or so earlier, and was found to contain at least seventeen grains of arsenic, some of which was to be seen undissolved, still in powder form, in his stomach. Seventeen grains would be enough to kill five or more grown, healthy men, if they had not previously been exposed to low levels of the metal and thus built up an immunity.

'Grains' here has nothing to do with granules or particles of arsenic: a grain is an old-fashioned measurement of weight, each grain being equal to .0648 of a modern metric gram. Grains are still used in the United States to indicate the amount of explosive enclosed in bullets. A level teaspoon of ordinary sugar weighs around sixty-two grains: since just three grains of arsenic is considered to be enough to kill a grown man in good health, then the arsenic equivalent in weight of a level teaspoon of sugar would be enough to kill twenty men.

The decisions to exhume Nattrass and the Cottons had been made after Mary Ann's magistrate's hearing at Bishop Auckland in August 1872. The evidence that these exhumations revealed caused three more hearings to be held at Bishop Auckland. Mary Ann Cotton was by now a celebrity, and people lined her route from Durham to

Bishop, hoping for a glimpse of the famous West Auckland poisoner.

At the end of the first hearing, Mary Ann was committed for trial at the next Durham assizes. Around this time, an investigation was begun into Mary Ann's past life. A report based on this investigation was sent to the Home Office by local police superintendent John Henderson on the first of October 1872. The report revealed that an unusual number of people who had lived with Mary Ann had died over the years, and that at least some of these deaths could have resulted from poisoning. According to Whitehead, the contents of this file were immediately leaked to the press; a questionable action that made a fair trial for Mary Ann rather less likely.

Mary Ann's trial at the Durham assizes was delayed when it was discovered that she was pregnant. There were at least two possible fathers for the child – the most likely candidates were the late Joseph Nattrass, and the bachelor Quick-Manning, the West Auckland brewery excise officer. Speculation about the identity of the father was dispelled when the baby was born on January 7th 1873, more than nine months after the death of Mary Ann's red-headed boyfriend. As if to settle the matter for good, Mary Ann named the baby Margaret Edith Quick-Manning Cotton. Since his own compound surname was extremely rare, there could be no mistake about Quick-Manning's responsibility for the child. Against the background of Victorian prudery, the fact must have made the poor excise officer's life a misery, at least for a while.

Margaret Edith was probably Mary Ann's twelfth child, and she was one of only two who survived her – the other was little George Robinson, born in 1869, the child Mary Ann abandoned and who eventually found his way back to his father James, Mary Ann's third husband.

Under normal circumstances, little Margaret Edith might have been taken on by her grandmother, once the authorities had satisfied themselves that Mary Ann's mother, Margaret Stott, bore no responsibility for any of her daughter's crimes. This could not, of course, have happened in Margaret Edith's case, since her grandmother was dead.

The prison-born baby was put up for adoption, and it is said that there were a hundred and fifty applications to adopt the child, one being from no less a personage than a Bishop Auckland J.P. For some reason, Mary Ann was able to choose which of the applicants would get the baby, and she chose Sarah and William Edwards, of Johnson Terrace, Mary Ann's old street in West Auckland. William worked as a coal-miner at St Helen Auckland, and the couple were childless after seven years of marriage.

Appleby was able to trace some of Margaret Edith's story and to interview her youngest son, Mary Ann Cotton's grandson. Sarah and William moved from West Auckland to the hamlet of Leasingthorne shortly after they adopted the baby, and there Margaret Edith *Edwards* was educated, married a miner and bore a daughter. The couple moved to the United States, to a coal-mining area near Boston, but Margaret Edith's husband was killed in an accident. Margaret Edith returned to County Durham, pregnant with her third child (a son had been born in the United States). Margaret Edith's third child, another son, was born in Low Spennymoor, and after she married another miner, a third son was born. This last son was the one Appleby was able to interview – he was a miner who retired in 1965. His two older half-brothers had both been killed in the First World War.

THE PICTURES

Some time during her stay in Durham gaol, Mary Ann was photographed. One of the paradoxes of her case is that, although during her life everyone saw her as a beauty, there is little in the way of good looks recorded in this one surviving photograph of her.

Since it was taken in the early 1870s, the picture was almost certainly taken by a professional photographer using the collodion wet-plate process. The glass plates that were used instead of film in this process had to be exposed and developed while still wet, so photographers needed a darkroom with developing equipment near their studios. If they were using their large, cumbersome wooden cameras out of doors, then they needed a tent or perhaps a specially-adapted coach in which to process the exposed plates.

Such cameras tended not to have shutters, so the exposure was made by removing the lens-cap for a few seconds and then replacing it. The lack of a shutter, and variations in the sensitivity of the coated plates, meant that it was tricky to get the exposure right, and the photograph of Mary Ann shows signs of having been over-exposed - this and the flat, even lighting means that there are barely any shadows on the face of the sitter, and her eye-brows are half bleached-out. Although exposure-times were very long by modern standards, the lens used here doesn't seem to have been good enough to record much detail - the camera also seems to have been focused on the wall behind the sitter, so that she seems slightly blurry. The photographer was probably aware of this problem once he'd developed his plate and printed the picture, but by then the sitter may have been long gone. Even for such a famous subject, he is not likely to have taken multiple shots so as to be able to pick a good one: the time and expense involved would have been prohibitive.

The picture is of course in black-and-white, or rather light and dark shades of brown, and this and the orthochromatic photography of the time - which didn't register all colours - tended to make the faces of caucasian sitters look dull and floury. Mary Ann's outfit also seems calculated to make her look plain, as it is excessively modest, and her chequered shawl makes her look hunched around the shoulders. The shawl and the ribbon tied under her chin obscure her neck, so we cannot tell from this picture if a swan-like neck was part of her charm. The shawl also prevents us from seeing much of the sitter's dress, which is a shame because some have speculated that her skill as a dress-maker allowed her to dress rather better than other people with her income. It is also possible that some of the money paid out to her from insurers and burial clubs went into good clothes, which would have added to her deadly attraction.

The combination of bonnet and hair-style are both unflattering, and Mary Ann has parted her hair slightly off-centre. There is no sign of make-up, which would have been unusual at this time in any case, and Mary Ann's pale-lipped mouth is open, as if for speech. We can't see her teeth, and her expression is anxious. Although the plate would have been exposed for just a few seconds, Mary Ann seems to have moved her hands during this time, or they may just be more out of focus than the rest of her. They seem to be large and strong, but with tapering fingers.

The light in the picture is consistent with its having come from a skylight or glass ceiling, such as were common in photographers' studios in those days. Photographic studio portraits from this period often featured pretty garden scenes painted on a canvas back-drop, or perhaps swags of heavy drapery, but the photographer here has chosen what looks like a smoothly-plastered and perhaps unpainted wall. The light would also be consistent with some out-door space within the prison, on a bright but overcast day.

In a modern outfit and with a modern hair-syle and make-up, the woman in the picture would pass unnoticed in County Durham today. This cannot be said for many of the celebrated beauties of Victorian times, who seem to have been rather stocky, short-necked and round-faced by modern standards. This change in the body-shape of women over the last hundred years or so is supposed to be due to changing

67

diet, and is one reason why modern people dressed in Victorian clothes and photographed with a Victorian camera seldom look entirely convincing as Victorians. Mary Ann's face is of a type regularly seen in the north-east, and its comparative length and slimness may have been part of Mary Ann's well-attested attractiveness.

The girl from Low Moorsley was a modern girl in ways other than just her appearance. Unlike the stereotypical Victorian woman she sought out sexual satisfaction, and seems to have targeted and seduced men – thus reversing the tradition whereby men were supposed to chase women. She also seems to have spent little time mourning for her dead husbands, children, lovers or mother – this at a time when mourning was supposed to be deep and lengthy: whole families of Victorians would dress themselves in black for years on end, and 'decent intervals' were endured before re-marriage. Mary Ann was also modern in that she was able to support herself independently by taking in lodgers and working as a nurse and house-keeper, at times when she was not formally connected to any man. This contrasts with the lives of many miners' wives in the twentieth century in County Durham, who did not work at all after marriage.

The photograph may have been taken when Mary Ann knew she was destined to hang, and anxiety over her fate would have written itself on her face. It seems that large numbers of copies of this photograph were sold as souvenirs around the time of Mary Ann's trial and execution.

The other picture of Mary Ann that is often seen seems to be an engraving prepared for an illustrated newspaper or magazine of the time. The woman in the picture looks quite unlike the Mary Ann in the photo – the only similarity is the glossy black hair. The woman in the engraving has her chin thrust forward in a way that challenges the viewer, and her eyes are cruelly narrowed. She has such high cheekbones that she looks like a lady from central Asia, and unfortunately the artist has made a mess of her nose. This melodramatic picture, which shows a rather mannish woman, ready for a fight, misses the point about Mary Ann – that her apparently gentle femininity made people trust her and think her harmless. The engraver was also seemingly unaware that people who do evil things are often the most ordinary-looking people in the world.

THE TRIAL

Many criminal trials are legally quite straightforward, but the trial of Mary Ann Cotton was marked by two tricky legal controversies. The first was to do with County Durham's historical status as the Land of the Prince Bishops, a separate kingdom within England, ruled by the Bishop of Durham.

William Van Mildert, the man who is usually identified as the last Prince Bishop of Durham, died in 1836, when Mary Ann Robson, as she then was, was just a little girl. In Victorian times some vestiges of the old County Palatine still existed in the legal system as it applied to County Durham, however, including the fact that the county had its own Attorney-General. In 1873 this was a Mr Aspinall, Recorder of Liverpool. Controversy arose when the Attorney-General for England, Sir John Duke Coleridge, went over Aspinall's head and appointed Charles Russell to lead for the prosecution against Mary Ann.

Coleridge's high-handed action caused offence and consternation in the north-east, and a question about this was asked in the House of Commons. The man who was supposed to answer the question, put by a Mr Wheelhouse, was none other than the future prime minister W.E. Gladstone. Then First Lord of the Treasury, Gladstone replied that the matter had nothing to do with him, and that he didn't understand it anyway. This was a case of Gladstone being a little economical with the truth, since it was the treasury that had to pay for Mary Ann Cotton's trial. Later, the Attorney-General admitted that it was the Treasury that had decided that Aspinall should be passed over.

Charles Arthur Russell, the leader for the prosecution, was an Irish Catholic with something of a hot temper and an aggressive style in cross-examining witnesses. He was forty at the time of the trial. His adversary, Thomas Campbell Foster, charged with the task of defending Mary Ann, was twenty years older but suffered from two disadvantages in this case – he accepted the job only two days before the start of the trial, and he got little or no help from Mary Ann's so-called solicitor, George Smith. Apart from taking her money and advising her to say nothing, Smith did hardly anything to help his client. He seems to have given up on her, believing that her case was hopeless. His inaction was highly unprofessional, and undermined the basis of criminal trials in England. We have an adversarial system, where the truth is supposed to be arrived at by two sides arguing the case. If one side can't be bothered, the system becomes distorted and unfit for purpose.

The second legal question that hung over the trial of Mary Ann Cotton was the matter of what evidence was admissible in court. The 'plan' for the trial was to consider evidence relating to the deaths of Charles Edward Cotton, his brother and his half-brother, and Joseph Nattrass: in other words, all those victims of Mary Ann Cotton whose bodies had been dug up and found to contain arsenic. To save time and money, the court would begin with Charles Edward, and leave off when and if enough evidence had been tested to convict Mary Ann of murder.

While Charles Edward's case was being considered, counsel for the prosecution started to bring in details relating to the cases of Nattrass, Frederick Cotton junior and Robert Robson Cotton. The defence counsel objected to this, and the judge retired to consider whether this 'extra' evidence was admissible. He concluded that it was, and Thomas Campbell Foster's job of defending the West Auckland Poisoner became even more difficult.

There are signs in the transcript of the trial that Campbell Foster was becoming a little desperate during the course of it. His main line of argument was that Charles Edward Cotton had ingested arsenic accidentally. Campbell Foster pounced on the fact that there was arsenical green wallpaper in the room where Charles Edward slept, ate and played, and made much of the fact that Mary Ann had cleaned the child's bed-frame with arsenic and soft soap.

Couldn't the child have dropped a piece of bread and butter on the floor, and then eaten the bread and butter which had acquired a coating of arsenic particles from the floor? Wasn't it true, Campbell Foster pointed out, that a piece of bread and butter dropped in this way always fell butter-down? And couldn't arsenic from the floor have been picked up by Charles Edward's toys?

Campbell Foster also asserted that particles of arsenic from the bed-frame, the wallpaper and the bed-sheets (which had been washed with arsenical soap) could have been inhaled by little Charles Edward, and thus poisoned him by slow degrees. He also suggested that the medicines he had been given in his last illness might have been mixed wrongly, and contained arsenic due to a ghastly error. Cambell Foster also reminded the jury that no arsenic had been found in Mary Ann's house after the murder had been committed.

Concluding his case for the defence, Campbell Foster reminded the jurors (who would have been all men at this time) of the special nature of mothers, who naturally cared for their little ones. Who could believe that a mother could do such a thing as to poison a child?

On the prosecution side, Charles Arthur Russell was able to establish by cross-examining the witnesses that Mary Ann had been cruel to little Charles Edward, had predicted his death, had obtained arsenic and had given the child everything he had had to eat and drink in his last days. It was also made clear that arsenic could easily be extracted from arsenical soft soap, simply by adding water to it. Russell reminded the jurors that poisoning was a crime easily prepared and perpetrated in secret, and that they shouldn't expect any witness to come forward and say that they'd actually seen Mary Ann in the act of poisoning little Charles Edward.

In his summing up, the Canadian-born judge, Thomas Dickson Archibald, reminded the jury that if they failed to see a reasonable motive for the child's murder, then they shouldn't be too concerned. Motive was often difficult to establish: what they should concentrate on was intention and action. He also defined the term 'reasonable doubt' for them – he warned them that they should not find Mary Ann not guilty because of a trivial doubt based on some minor inconsistency in the evidence. The judge also asserted that he had been completely right in allowing information about three other deaths to permeate Mary Ann's trial for the murder of her step-son.

After deliberating for less than an hour, the jury returned a unanimous verdict of guilty. Technically, this applied only to the murder of Charles Edward Cotton, but by now everyone knew about Mary Ann's past, and many considered her guilty of a far greater number of murders than those she is supposed to have inflicted on the unfortunate Cotton family. Mary Ann was considered to be what we would now call a serial killer.

MARY ANN'S RIVALS

A serial killer is defined as an individual who has killed three or more people over a period of more than a month, with a 'cooling-off period' between each. The motivation for the killings is usually psychological gratification. Serial killers must be differentiated from mass murderers, who kill multiple people at one time, and spree killers, who murder people in two or more locations without a break.

Due in part to the rarity of female murderers, Mary Ann Cotton's case was considered unique and shocking at the time, and her actions seemed unprecedented and inexplicable. She was not, however, the only female serial killer, or the first. Many other women have killed multiple times.

One famous female serial killer, now almost a creature of folklore, was Elizabeth Báthory of Hungary. She has been dubbed 'Lady Dracula' and 'The Blood Countess'. Between 1590 and 1610, Báthory and four collaborators were said to have tortured and killed six hundred and fifty young girls at her home, Sárvár Castle. Witnesses claimed that the daughters of local peasants were lured to the castle with offers of work as maidservants, while daughters of lesser gentry were sent to learn courtly manners. The crimes that were committed there were said to have included beatings, mutilation, cannibalism, starvation and sexual abuse.

Some claim that the accusations against Báthory were motivated by sectarian politics, as she was a powerful Protestant aristocrat in a time of religious conflict. A myth emerged (first recorded by a scholar called László Turóczi in 1769) that the countess bathed in her victim's blood to retain her youth and beauty; but the motive of sadistic pleasure was suggested as more plausible by historians at the beginning of the nineteenth century. The myth of Elizabeth Báthory is a constant draw for tourists to eastern Europe, and serves as an inspiration for similar characters in books, music, plays and films.

Mary Ann Cotton's crimes can be placed in perspective by research into other female multiple murderers. Her *modus operandi* was typically female: the *Electronic journal of sociology* (published by the University of Guelph, Ontario) estimates that eighty percent of female serials killers have used poison. Cotton's crimes were undetected from 1864 to 1872 – this fits in with the average of six to eight years that elapses before female killers are apprehended by the police. In his book *Serial murderers and their victims*, Eric Hickey explains this with the observation that females are 'quiet killers'; they employ subtle means, and are sly, deliberate and careful. Their style contrasts with that of male killers, who typically kill violently, commonly stabbing, battering or strangling, and are usually discovered within an average of four years, with some serial killers being stopped after only four months.

In her time, Mary Ann Cotton was dubbed 'Cottonmouth' after a venomous snake, and also 'Lady Rotten'. After her death, she was one of the first killers to be called a 'black widow', a phrase which has become a common categorisation for a certain variety of female serial murderers. The phrase is derived from a species of toxic spider, the female of which kills its mates when they are no longer useful. As opposed to the sexual motivation of some male serial killers, black widows commonly murder for money, living off insurance policies, pensions and legacies given to them after the deaths of close friends and relatives.

Black widows are the most notorious type of female serial killers, but eight other categorisations were identified by the Kellehers in their book *Murder most rare: the female serial killer*, including 'angels of death', 'sexual predators', 'revenge killers', 'profit killers' and 'team killers'.

An 'angel of death' commonly kills people she has decided are already destined for extinction, such as an ageing relative or a patient in a hospital. Typical means of killing are lethal injections or suffocation with a pillow. An example of this type of killer is Beverly Allit. Like Cotton, she was an English nurse, working on the children's ward of Grantham and Kesteven Hospital in Lincolnshire.

75

From February to April 1991 she attempted to kill thirteen children (succeeding in four cases) by lethally injecting them with potassium chloride or insulin. Her victims' ages ranged from seven weeks to eleven years, and all were admitted to the ward with minor health problems, only to suffer from mysterious cardiac arrests or hypoglycaemia within days.

Ironically, the parents of victim Katie Phillips were so grateful for their nurse's care that they asked Allit to be her godmother. Katie survived, but suffered permanent brain damage, partial paralysis and partial blindness. Allit was charged with attempted murder and grievous bodily harm in November 1991, and sentenced to thirteen life sentences. The motives for her crimes are not entirely clear, but it has been suggested that her actions may be explained by Munchausen syndrome by proxy, a disorder in which a person fakes an illness in someone in their care in order to attract attention and sympathy for themselves. This contrasts with straightforward Munchausen syndrome, where sufferers fake diseases in themselves.

One of the most notorious recent serial killers, Aileen Wuornos, has been called a sexual predator. She had a difficult childhood. Her father was a schizophrenic, in prison for the rape and attempted murder of an eight year old boy. Aileen never met him, and he committed suicide in prison in 1969. Her mother left her and her siblings in the care of their grandparents before Aileen reached the age of four. She claimed that her grandfather sexually abused her, and she became pregnant at fourteen after being raped by one of his friends. The baby was given up for adoption, and Aileen was thrown out of the house at fifteen to support herself as a prostitute.

In the following years she was frequently arrested, on charges such as armed robbery, car theft and assault and battery. In 1989 she committed her first murder; shooting Richard Mallory in his car in self-defence after he violently raped her. She killed six more in the next year; soliciting men, shooting them after intercourse and stealing their cars and belongings. She was sentenced to death in 1992, and after ten years on death row was finally executed by lethal injection.

Her categorisation as a sexual predator has been challenged.

Wuornos was a lesbian, in a relationship with a hotel maid called Tyria Moore, which makes it less likely that her killings were driven by the urge to fulfil a sexual fantasy. A desire for revenge against men may have motivated her, or her desperate financial situation may have made theft seem like a necessity. Nick Broomfield, the director of the documentary *Aileen: life and death of a serial killer* stated: 'I think this anger developed inside her...[when] she was working as a prostitute. I think this anger just spilled out from inside her, and finally exploded into incredible violence. That was her way of surviving'.

Revenge killers are as rare as sexual predators, and kill out of love, hate and jealousy. They are commonly obsessed with their target and seek vengeance. Martha Hasel was born in Ohio in 1884, to a poor farming family. After an abusive marriage with a man twenty years her senior, she was left with four children when her husband Albert Wise died. She found a new lover in the shape of Walter Johns, a much younger man, but her family disapproved of the match. After many bitter arguments, members of her family began dying of 'stomach inflammation'. It transpired that Martha had killed three family members with cyanide in revenge for their objections to her alliance with Johns. The jury took an hour to convict her of first degree murder, and she died in prison in 1971.

Stereotypically, hired assassins are seen as male; expert and merciless, they kill for money. 'Hit women' do, however, exist, and are categorised as profit killers. Usually, jealous wives hire these professional women to eliminate a cheating husband. Madame Alexe Popova of Russia hated to see peasant wives trapped in abusive marriages, and created a service for her neighbours: she would poison their husbands for a small fee. She killed three hundred men from 1879 to 1909. When in custody, she stated that she 'did excellent work in freeing unhappy wives from their tyrants' and she had 'never killed a woman'. She was still unrepentant when she was executed by firing squad (despite attempts by a mob to burn her at the stake). As profit killers are seldom connected to their victims, their careers can continue undetected for many years.

Two thirds of female serial killings take place within a team. The

77

most common type of team is a male/female duo, who are often lovers seeking sexual thrills. Ian Brady and Myra Hindley are an example of this, as well as Rose and Fred West. In these types of partnership, women are often controlled by the man they love, coerced into helping him fulfil sexual fantasies in fear of his abandonment.

Male dominance is also seen in 'killing families' such as the Manson family, who made headlines in the 1960s. Charles Manson established himself as the leader of his own cult, and this group went on to commit the ritual murder of actress Sharon Tate and nineteen others. Cotton overturns this power play; killing independently and controlling men for her own gain before disposing of them.

Female-female 'kill teams' also exist in defiance of convention, as demonstrated by the case of Helen Golay and Olga Rutterschmidt, who were convicted in 2008. Both women were in their seventies, and took in homeless men from the streets of Hollywood, taking care of them for two years while taking out large insurance policies. When the time period needed to contest that the policies were fraudulent expired, the pair drugged the men, drove them to a secluded alley and ran over them with their car until they were dead. Golay collected more than one and a half million dollars from a single pay-out, and described homeless people as 'parasitic' and 'useless to society'. The media was shocked by the fact that two 'little old ladies' could be capable of such cold-blooded killing.

Helen and Olga are reminiscent of the two old ladies in Joseph Kesselring's 1939 play *Arsenic and old lace*, which was adapted for the cinema by Frank Capra in 1944. In the play, the two elderly aunts of the hero kill lonely old men with poisoned home-made elderberry wine.

Cotton's black widow status defies the stereotypical female role in society in many ways. Black widows kill the husbands they are supposed to love and serve, and sometimes kill their own children, perverting the idealistic image of a doting and selfless mother. This is part of what makes Cotton's case so disturbing. In *Murder most rare*, the Kellehers state that 'because she will deliberately target those who have come to trust her, the crimes of this type of serial murderer

78

violate our basic assumptions about love, loyalty, guardianship and friendship'.

The majority of black widows begin killing in their thirties: if Cotton killed her first husband in 1864 when she was 32, then she fits the stereotype. Some estimate that she killed eighteen people: slightly higher than the black widow average of ten to fifteen. The murders are usually well-planned and methodical; Cotton worked her way through four husbands, received their life insurance and inheritance, and moved house frequently to avoid suspicion.

Though only one of many black widows throughout history, Cotton was one of the first to be recognised as such, and her dubious achievement may have been due to an assortment of historical factors which made her task relatively easy. Forensic science in Victorian times was in its infancy, and not much used by the police to apprehend criminals. The bodies of murder victims were often left unexamined, and only highly suspicious cases were thought to warrant investigation. This may have contributed to the frequent diagnosis of typhoid or gastric fever in Cotton's victims. The Victorian attitude to women tended to exclude the possibility that these delicate creatures could kill. Women's gentle virtues were placed on a pedestal, and the deaths of Mary Ann Cotton's nearest and dearest would have evoked sympathy rather than misgivings in many conventionally-minded men.

DEATH ROW

By modern standards, the three-day trial that sent Mary Ann Cotton to the scaffold was hurried and ill-prepared. There were more witnesses who could have been called, including expert witnesses with specialist skills and knowledge. Inconsistencies in evidence were not followed up: these included the fact that, though Dr Kilburn asserted that there had been no arsenic in powder form in his dispensary, his assistant, Dr Archibald Chalmers, disagreed. If Chalmers was right, then it was more likely that arsenic had been mixed into one of Charles Edwards' medicines by mistake.

The state of forensic science at the time was decidedly primitive, and one feels that Dr Scattergood's total confidence in the results of his own tests may have been misplaced. The lack of other specialist experts meant that, as a medical man, Dr Kilburn was asked to give his opinion on all sorts of matters (including arsenic wallpaper) about which, as a village doctor, he might have known very little.

Scattergood's assertions were questioned in no less a place than Britain's premier medical journal, *The Lancet*. In an article in the edition of March 15th 1873, the author stated, as Mary Ann's defence counsel had done, that particles of arsenic breathed in from the air could stick to the back of the throat and be swallowed, ending up in the stomach. *The Lancet* also reminded its readers that arsenic dust, absorbed through the lungs, could cause inflammation in various parts of the body, including the digestive system. The author of the article was of the opinion that, given Mary Ann's past, the verdict passed against her was probably the right one, but remarked on the relative slightness of the evidence upon which it was based.

From the medical point of view, it might have been better to try Mary Ann first for the murder of Nattrass, in whose body a far more damning quantity of arsenic was found. Nattrass's death had, however, happened earlier than Charles Edward's, and perhaps it would have been harder to find witnesses with accurate memories of what had happened then. Nattrass's body would also have been more decayed, and less likely to yield evidence other than the quantity of arsenic.

People who believe that capital punishment should be re-introduced in Britain sometimes assume that people living in the country when this ultimate punishment was still used regarded it as a perfectly justifiable, even natural, thing. This was certainly not the case. Despite the lurid stories about her crimes that had been circulating in the press, a number of petitions and private letters were sent to the Home Office, calling for mercy in the case of Mary Ann Cotton.

John T. Nixon, a Darlington solicitor, wrote a letter to the Home Office which was signed by a hundred and thirty people from Darlington and Bishop Auckland. Those who signed were from a variety of stations in life, from 'gentleman' to 'labourer'.

Nixon's letter expressed the concern that, because Mary Ann's defence was so poorly organised, there had been no experts to put up against Dr Thomas Scattergood, whose assertions swept away the concerns of the other witnesses. Nixon was also concerned that bottles were known to have disappeared from the house in Front Street, West Auckland before the police had a chance to analyse their contents. Sergeant Hutchinson, the investigating officer, had assumed that these had belonged to Dr Kilburn, and that he had reclaimed them. When asked about this, Kilburn said he hadn't taken them. In theory, if these bottles had been analysed, they could have proved that Mary Ann had been given arsenic by mistake.

The philanthropic Quaker Edward Backhouse, who had employed Mary Ann, sent another letter to the Home Office, asking for a reprieve for her on the basis that the evidence against her was so threadbare. Various people who had known her or worked with her in Sunderland put their names to the letter. Backhouse later sent another letter with a similar argument: neither of these letters, sponsored by one of Sunderland's leading personalities, had any effect. In his second letter, addressed to a Mr Tallack at the Home Office,

Backhouse used the old-fashioned sounding 'thou' and 'thee' instead of 'you' - a characteristic of the Plain Quaker speech of the time: 'Canst thou do what is in thy power to represent these things'.

Backhouse later sent a telegraph to the Home Secretary, promising to send him several local newspapers, the contents of which, he hoped, would change the government's mind.

The other Quakers of Sunderland sent a separate petition, with forty-nine signatures. The Sunderland architect Frank Caws sent his own letter, claiming that Mary Ann may have killed Nattrass and the three Cottons by dosing them with arsenic in an attempt to cure pre-existing illnesses such as typhoid. On a touchingly human and practical level, a Martha Olive of Dorchester implied in her letter that Mary Ann should not be executed until her child was weaned. This argument will seem very forceful to us in the twenty-first century: in recent years, the reputation of the mother's breast-milk as the best food for babies has risen exponentially.

Mary Ann herself wrote a series of letters from death row. In these, she asserted her innocence, lamented the supposed mistakes that had led to her being condemned to death, and begged friends and relatives to visit her and work to save her from the noose. She was particularly scornful about her solicitor George Smith, whose advice to her to keep her mouth shut in court had turned out not to be good advice at all.

The letters were printed as written in various newspapers of the time, and these reproductions show that, although she had been a Sunday school teacher, Mary Ann had little grasp of spelling, punctuation or capitalisation. Her spelling provides some clues as to how she spoke. She wrote 'meet' as 'meeat', 'aunt' as 'ant' and 'there' as 'thore'. These and other spellings suggest that, as we would expect, Mary Ann spoke with a north-east, more specifically a Wearside, accent.

Although her letters show some signs that she was trying to write in a formal way, Mary Ann often used words and phrases that reflect her northern working-class background. She used 'wrote' instead of 'written', 'childer' instead of 'children' and the phrase 'they call him' instead of 'he is called' or 'his name is', which is still a feature of the

Wearside dialect.

Mary Ann's poor spelling was referred to by George Stott, her stepfather and one of her last visitors in prison. He expressed some disappointment about the spelling, told Mary Ann that none of the petitions she had heard about had been presented (which was untrue) and tried to impress her with the gravity of her situation. Mary Ann's visitors and correspondents at this time tried to get her to face up to her crimes and to confess. This, they thought, would lighten the weight of her guilt in the scales kept by God. She was visited by Methodist ministers who tried to comfort her and advise her in this time of extreme fear. One of them, called Stevenson, became convinced that Mary Ann Cotton was innocent.

Mary Ann continued to maintain her innocence of any crime except for the bigamous marriage to Frederick Cotton and the fact that her last baby had therefore been born out of wedlock. She asserted that the poison had been accidentally mixed into some arrowroot sold to her by a grocer at West Auckland. It is possible that this arrowroot, if it ever existed, had been sold from a shop owned by Mary Ann's nemesis, Thomas Riley. Arrowroot is still used by some people as a remedy for stomach complaints, particularly diarrhoea.

When William and Mary Edwards came for little Margaret Edith, they brought with them William Lowrey, Mary Ann's last lodger. Lowrey wrote an account of his visit for the local *Northern Echo* newspaper, in which he revealed that the conditions in which the prisoner was living out her last days were 'fifty times better' than he had expected. The female warders of the prison had given up their retiring-room for her; a clean, well-lit room with 'pretty paper' on the walls, a good fire, a bed, table and chairs. Two warders stayed with Mary Ann at all times.

Another Mary

If we give credence to her tale about the arrowroot, then the faint possibility appears that Mary Ann may not have been a serial killer, but just a very unlucky woman, many of whose friends and relatives died before their time – often of typhoid, or symptoms of typhoid such as diarrhoea.

Readers with some knowledge of the history of medicine might be reminded, at this point, of the strange case of Mary Mallon, known as 'Typhoid Mary', a typhoid carrier who was discovered in Oyster Bay, New York in 1904. Mallon was a cook with, it seems, no sense of personal hygiene or cleanliness, and she may have been responsible for three or more deaths from typhoid before she was eventually forced into quarantine on North Brother Island, New York. Could Mary Ann Cotton have been a typhoid carrier like Mary Mallon?

Appleton briefly entertains the idea that Mary Ann Cotton may have been using arsenic as a medicine, and it is possible that she may have got into the habit of doing this because so many people she lived with seemed to go down with typhoid. She may have regarded arsenic as a cure for this disease, and been reluctant to explain this to her accusers. She may have kept quiet about it because it would have meant admitting that she *had* obtained arsenic and administered it to those who had died when they lived with her. As far as we know, she didn't tell any of the doctors in attendance that she was doing this, but then she might have been embarrassed by the fact that she had foolishly given her 'patients' too much arsenic.

The idea that Mary Ann Cotton was a typhoid carrier is particularly attractive because all the people Mary Ann is supposed to have killed were people for whom she would have prepared food. Typhoid transmits extremely well through uncooked food (Typhoid Mary's

peach ice cream was supposed to be particularly risky) and Mary
Ann Cotton would undoubtedly have prepared cold meals featuring
bread, butter, dripping, jam, ham and cheese for her husbands,
boyfriends and children.

Cooking hot food would have been very time-consuming given the
equipment of the time, which relied on heat from coal, not the more
convenient gas or electricity. As a housewife who may have been
unenthusiastic about domestic labour, Mary Ann may have been
making up cold collations on a regular basis. With no ice-box or
refrigerator, the typhoid bacilli would have multiplied very quickly,
particularly on and in meat and milk products.

Mary Ann's houses would sometimes have been very dirty by
modern standards, and the lady herself may not have washed herself,
or even her hands, very often. With no running hot water, every drop
of hot water in the house would have had to be heated up, so that the
simple business of washing her hands with soap in warm water might
have taken Mary such a long time that it would hardly have seemed
worth it.

Although Mary Ann is accused of having killed a number of small
babies, it is interesting to note that the death-certificates of these
infants, as re-printed by Whitehead, do not show the cause of death
to be typhoid or anything like it. If we take the 'typhoid carrier'
theory seriously, we might conclude that Mary Ann's children had to
be at least weaned before they could die of typhoid, because typhoid
is only very rarely transmitted via breast-milk. Once they were on
solid food, they were in more danger.

A further indicator that there might be something in this theory is
the fact that Mary Ann's mother only died when Mary Ann was
looking after her. This care would no doubt have included the
preparation of food. When Margaret was cooking for her daughter,
and not the other way round, she would have been much safer. By
the same token, the female warders who attended to Mary Ann in
prison would not have contracted the disease, because their prisoner
was probably not preparing any food for them.

The idea of Cotton as a typhoid carrier would not have occurred to
any of the physicians involved in her case because the existence of

such carriers, who pass on the disease but are not themselves ill, was not discovered until some years after Mary Ann's death. The discovery was made by Dr Robert Koch, the bald, bearded and bespectacled genius of early microbiology. The typhoid germ itself was not identified until 1880, so it would have been impossible to test Mary Ann for typhoid germs during her life – the disease could only be diagnosed by its symptoms before 1880.

It may be that Mary Ann's life as a typhoid carrier (who could not have known of her condition) had made her accustomed to seeing the slow agonising deaths of everyone she cared for. Her heart may have hardened and, thinking that all her family members were fated to die (and with an eye to the insurance money) she may have been tempted to hurry them away with poison.

That other Mary, the typhoid carrier Mary Mallon, found it hard to accept what she was, even though some of the most eminent experts in the country explained it to her. This is why Typhoid Mary started cooking again, for hospital patients, before she was recaptured and returned to quarantine. Mary Ann Cotton could never have been told that she was a typhoid carrier, and she may indeed have seen the visits of typhoid to her house as bad luck, or even a punishment for her sins. She may even have regarded herself as spiritually doomed and eternally 'dirty' as soon as she engaged in pre-marital sex with William Mowbray.

DEATH BY HANGING

Mary Mallon's sentence was to remain in relative isolation in her filthy bungalow on North Brother island until she died of natural causes. Mary Ann Cotton's fate was more barbaric, and rather quicker in coming. William Calcraft, Mary Ann's elderly and incompetent hangman, arrived in Durham on the afternoon of Saturday 22nd of March. He had been in Durham on his shameful business two months earlier, when he had hanged Hugh Slane and John Hays of Spennymoor – these men had been sentenced to hang because they had kicked one Joseph Wain to death. For Hays and Slane, the gallows had been set up over a steep-sided pit, so that as the trap-door opened the men seemed to fall into the earth. The pit was still there for Mary Ann's execution, and the scaffold was reconstructed over it.

Robert Anderson Evans (or Evens) assisted Calcraft. He was a Welshman, from Carmarthen, who had trained at first as a physician. Like Calcraft, he preferred to use the short-drop method for hanging, which risked the victim hanging at the end of the rope for minutes on end, dying of slow strangulation. In 1874 Evans hanged the last woman in Britain to be hanged by this method – Mary Anne Barry. This Mary Anne – who unlike Mary Ann Cotton spelt her middle name with an 'e', had been found guilty of poisoning a baby, an act which she had successfully carried out together with one Edwin Bailey, who may have been her lover. The pair were hanged at Gloucester together with Edward Butt, another murderer whose crime was not connected to theirs.

As in some of William Calcraft's hangings, Mary Anne Barry continued to struggle at the end of the rope for some time, and Evans had to push down on her shoulders to finish the job.

Hangings of women were rare – such a thing had not happened at

Durham since before Calcraft was born. Mary Nicholson was hanged – twice – in 1799. The first time, the rope broke, and the prisoner recovered sufficiently to talk to her relatives. It took nearly an hour for a new rope to be brought. Nicholson was a servant who had been found guilty of killing her mistress, Elizabeth Atkinson, at Little Stainton (just west of Stockton-on-Tees) in 1798. Mary is supposed to have killed Elizabeth by adding poison to a pudding.

Arthur Appleton's description of Mary Ann Cotton's hanging is direct, detailed and heart-breaking. These were the days before the specially-constructed condemned cells of the last years of hanging in Britain. Such cells had false walls that were pulled aside so that the prisoner suddenly found himself in the execution chamber. The last hangings in England were supposedly quick and humane, leading to a near-instantaneous death. For Mary Ann's generation, there was still the grim procession from cell to pinioning-room, then out to the scaffold in an open-air part of the prison, then the short drop and the chance of a death by agonizingly slow strangulation. This is exactly what happened to Mary Ann Cotton – she struggled for three minutes at the end of the rope before her body became still. In keeping with tradition, the body was left hanging for an hour before it was taken down.

A cast was made of Mary Ann's head, and this was submitted to the phrenological societies of Hartlepool and Edinburgh. Phrenologists (or 'bump feelers') believed that a person's personality was reflected in the shape of his or her head. The bump-feelers of Edinburgh declared that Mary Ann was 'a thoroughly criminal type' while those at Hartlepool said that her skull betrayed a lack of morals, and strong animal urges. According to Derek Hebden, the Hartlepool phrenologists also detected tell-tale signs of 'coarseness, vulgarity, destructiveness, secretiveness, self-reliance, firmness, benevolence and evil' and added that the subject must have been fond of both 'hard work and the good life'. Hartlepool's Theatre Royal later hosted a play called *The great moral drama of the life and death of Mary Ann Cotton*, with a Miss Leighton in the title role.

Doubts remained (as they still do) about whether or not Mary Ann Cotton was guilty. The murders she is supposed to have committed before she came to West Auckland were never fully investigated, and none of the bodies were ever exhumed for analysis. The bodies of the four people Mary Ann is supposed to have killed at West Auckland all had arsenic in them, but Mary Ann's inquest and trial, and the investigations that led up to them, were all too quick and confused to establish her guilt or innocence definitively. There certainly were other ways that arsenic could have got into the children, and the large amount of arsenic found inside Joseph Nattrass could have got there by over-zealous dosing with the poison to cure some ailment, or because Nattrass was a habitual arsenic-eater, who believed, like the Styrians, that the poison would make him strong and virile.

As if to demonstrate that the legal system of the time was not keen to reform itself in the light of Mary Ann Cotton's botched treatment, Elizabeth Pearson, also a poisoner, was hanged at Durham in 1874 after a trial lasting just a day. Again the judge was the Canadian Thomas Dickson Archibald, and again the forensic expert Thomas Scattergood presented his findings to the court. Like Mary Anne Barry, Elizabeth Pearson was hanged together with two men. This time, the short drop was not used – the executioner, William Marwood, was a pioneer of the long drop, by which, in theory, the neck was instantly broken.

The West Auckland Fair and Cattle Show of 1873 featured a waxwork model of Mary Ann Cotton, which must have been hard to look at, for those who had known her. The waxwork was displayed very near Mary Ann's old house in the village.

Whatever the doubts surrounding her case, Mary Ann Cotton, the West Auckland Poisoner, became a celebrity in the north-east prior to her death, and is still well-known, especially among County Durham people, to this day. A rhyme about her, reproduced at the front of this book, is still recited, and parents used to use her name to frighten children, much as they had once used the name of Napoleon Bonaparte.

The folklore version of Mary Ann seems to have broken loose from the true version some time ago. It is commonly held that she lured strangers' children into her house with the promise of sweets, which turned out to be laced with poison. This version of Mary Ann puts her in the same class as Baba Yaga, the evil witch of Russian fairy-tales. This was of course not Mary Ann's style: like most murderers, she kept her crime within the family.

Outside of the north-east of England, Mary Ann is less well-known, possibly because her reputation as a Victorian serial-killer is eclipsed by that of Jack the Ripper. Jack has the advantage as a celebrity because his identity is still unknown and therefore mysterious, and because his murders took place in London, the great Victorian city of Sherlock Holmes, hansom cabs, gas-light and 'pea-souper' fogs. The Ripper's victims were adult prostitutes, and it is perhaps easier to think about adults being murdered than defenceless children and babies. In terms of numbers killed, however, the Ripper murders were a minor phenomenon in comparison to Mary Ann's possible death-toll. There were five 'canonical' Ripper murders, but at least one of these is thought by experts to have been committed by someone other than Jack himself.

Madwoman or Monster?
A Diagnosis of Mary Ann Cotton

It is natural to ask, exactly how many did Mary Ann Cotton kill? It is impossible to answer this question. We only have something resembling proper evidence about four deaths, and, as we have seen, this evidence can be interpreted a number of ways. There was no confession forthcoming from Mary Ann, right up to the moment of her death, despite the efforts of friends, relations and spiritual advisers to obtain such a confession from her. If, however, we accept that just one of the West Auckland deaths was caused by Mary Ann, then we open up the possibility that she was responsible for at least some of the many deaths that seemed to surround her during her life.

It is tempting to blame Mary Ann for the deaths of any of her house-mates who died of anything like typhoid because, as *The Lancet* mentioned in connection with the Cotton case, it was difficult to distinguish the symptoms of typhoid from those of arsenic poisoning. The Victorians were, however, dying of typhoid and similar diseases all the time, and it is unlikely that a woman of Mary Ann Cotton's class, living at that time, could have borne twelve or more children and had four husbands and a mother without at least some of them succumbing to typhoid, gastric fever, English or Asian cholera, or similar diseases.

The maximum number of murders attributed to Mary Ann is twenty-one or twenty-two, the slight vagueness in the number being because nobody knows exactly how many children she gave birth to in the west country. This high number cannot be accurate, because it includes deaths by, for instance, typhus, the symptoms of which are distinct from those of typhoid and arsenic poisoning.

If we believe that Mary Ann Cotton deliberately killed ten or more of her unfortunate relatives, then we must look for a reason for her repeated murderous behaviour. Can it be that her crimes were so pitiless and motiveless that we must conclude that she was mentally ill? Mary Ann was not tested for madness during her imprisonment, and her behaviour did not show any florid manifestations of mental disorder. It may, nevertheless, be possible to diagnose such a condition retrospectively. This process does not involve finding an excuse for Mary Ann's actions, but it may be that some part of her brain function was so impaired that we cannot think of her *choosing* to commit terrible crimes, any more than a woman with a broken ankle *chooses* to limp.

Psychological problems can weaken a person's self-control, increase the strength of their urges and create an unstable state of mind.

The most common psychological term experts use when describing a serial killer is 'psychopath'. This word describes a person with a mental disorder known as antisocial personality disorder. The disorder includes a number of traits which surround a general disregard for the welfare of others. Psychopaths or sociopaths cannot empathise with other people, or feel emotional towards them, and will manipulate them for their own ends, finding it difficult to feel guilt or remorse. Within the modern justice system in the United States, a psychopath may be able to pass lie-detector tests, and will often justify his crimes with claims of amnesia or temporary insanity. A psychopath may also attempt to pose as an authority figure such as a doctor or teacher, aided by his ability to charm and deceive others.

A diagnosis of antisocial personality disorder does not mean that a person will inevitably become a violent criminal or serial killer. When sociopaths realise that their minds work differently from other people's minds, they can force themselves to think and act like the normal people they see around them. In fact many sociopaths live and work comfortably in society, even getting married and starting families. The traits of a psychopath can, however, make for an efficient murderer, coupled with the superficial charisma that allows some psychopaths to gain the trust of others. The serial killer Ted Bundy is an example of a superficially charming psychopathic murderer; he killed thirty women in five years, using his charm to win their trust before remorselessly strangling or beating them to death.

Mary Ann Cotton could easily be called a psychopath; she may have remorselessly killed husbands, her own children and her mother. Her charm was also recorded, with witnesses at her trial mentioning her beauty and winning personality.

There is another way to approach the psychology of serial killers, not through patterns in their behaviour and thought, but through the activity in their brains. Neurological explanations seek to find a connection between the balance of chemicals in the brain, and an individual's actions. Violent behaviour is associated with the neurotransmitter system. Neurotransmitters are chemicals which transmit electrical signals across synapses in the brain. Certain neurotransmitters inhibit a person's behaviour, making them less likely to breach social norms and act violently. These include serotonin and GABA (gamma aminobutryric acid). Other neurotransmitters are excitatory, meaning that they provoke wilder behaviour and strong emotions. These include acetylcholine and norepinephrine.

When there is a lack of inhibitory neurotransmitters, an individual experiences 'disinhibition' of brain functions. This means that the neurons (nerve cells which transmit electrical signals) are firing too much, leading to instability which can be expressed in violent outbursts. We know that Mary Ann was capable of physical violence: her treatment of little Charles Edward Cotton went beyond even Victorian norms of corporal punishment within the home. It is interesting that Mary Ann didn't moderate this violent behaviour when witnesses were present – which is how we know about it. Of course the sudden rage that may lead to the violent beating of a child is different from the quiet, slow-burning emotion that may compel someone to plan to poison another human being.

As well as chemicals like acetylcholine and norepinephrine, hormones may also have a part to play in encouraging murderous behaviour. The hormone serotonin regulates the activity of the limbic system, which is an area of the brain which creates emotional behaviour, including aggression. If serotonin levels are too low, the limbic system processes without restriction, causing vivid and uncontrollable emotions. A lower amount of serotonin may be a result of genetic factors, a poor diet, or lesions in the brain. A person experiencing this impairment may have reduced impulse control, so they may become a slave to their violent urges.

Hormone imbalances such as these can be caused by brain defects at birth, or by a head injury. The killer Bobby Joe Long suffered damage to his head in a motorcycle accident, and went on to rape and murder ten women in Florida. At the time of writing, Long is still on death row. A head injury can damage the hypothalamus, a part of the brain which controls the hormonal system and, in turn, the emotions.

Any of the factors described above could have contributed to Mary Ann Cotton's brutal crimes, but a lack of medical analysis and the limited knowledge of how the brain worked at the time means that certainty is impossible. Modern neuroscientists would be as interested in the structures and chemicals inside Mary Ann's brain as the phrenologists of Hartlepool were in the bumps on her skull.

A biological approach like the analysis of the brain may seem to ignore aspects of a criminal's life which may lead to crime. Studies of recent American serial killers suggest that their violent behaviour may originate from two social influences: a 'culture of violence' that changes the state of mind of an individual, and childhood experience. The idea of a culture of violence can be applied to modern America due to the violent role-models seen in films and television, as well as the idealisation of masculine traits of aggression and dominance. This idea can also be applied to Victorian England.

Mary Ann Cotton grew up in the harsh working-class environment of the mining villages of County Durham. Crime was common, and regulated rather haphazardly by the agents of the law. As we have seen, death was also ever-present due to high rates of infection from diseases such as typhoid and cholera. In short, human life was more fleeting, and perhaps regarded as less precious. The cultural context that Cotton experienced may have made it easier for her to contemplate the crimes of infanticide and homicide.

Her early experiences may also have shaped Mary Ann's later actions. As a young child, she lost her father in an accident, an event which plunged her family into poverty. Her mother worked hard to support Mary and her siblings, keeping them from life in the workhouse.

The loss of her father may have cost her an important attachment in her life. The emotional connection that forms between parents and children can have a profound effect on an individual's attitude to herself and the world. As the fatherly bond was lost, and that of the mother disrupted by the need to work, Cotton may have become detached and unable to feel sympathy, affection or guilt.

Detached children are known to form one-sided relationships merely to satisfy their own needs, and are more likely to display aggressive behaviour. These traits can be seen in Cotton: it could be argued that she connected herself with men for personal gain, and seemed to feel no remorse after murdering them. In fact, the common factor of a lack of nurturing contact in childhood is seen in many more contemporary serial killers including Ted Bundy, Charles Manson and Ian Brady.

Her experiences of poverty may also have encouraged Mary Ann to attempt to achieve material comfort at any price, even killing those who got in the way of her quest for the ideal lifestyle. This makes the story of Mary Ann Cotton's life read like a tragic version of the children's rhyme, *Michael Finnegan*. Like poor Michael, Mary Ann repeatedly felt compelled to begin again.

SELECT BIBLIOGRAPHY

Appleton, Arthur: *Mary Ann Cotton: Her story and trial*, County Durham Books, 1996

Begg, Paul, Fido, Martin and Skinner, Paul: *The complete Jack the Ripper A-Z*, John Blake, 2010

Bourdain, Anthony: *Typhoid Mary*, Bloomsbury, 2001

Carlton, C.M.: *History of the charities in the city of Durham*, George Walker, 1872

Conyers Surtees, H: *The history of the parish and township of St Helen Auckland together with the township of West Auckland*, 1924

Flaubert, Gustave: *Madame Bovary* (trans. Eleanor Marx-Aveling), IAPP, 2011

Frost, Ginger: *Living in sin: Cohabiting as husband and wife in nineteenth-century England*, Manchester University Press, 2008

Hadas, Moses and Mclean, John: *Ten plays by Euripides*, Bantam, 1981

Hardy, Thomas: *Jude the obscure*, Oxford, 2009

Hebden, Derek J.: *Murder at West Auckland: Mary Ann Cotton*, Derek Hebden, 1987

Hickey, Eric W.: *Serial murderers and their victims*, Wadsworth, 2005

Hodge, James A: *Famous trials III*, Penguin, 1950

Isichei, Elizabeth: *Victorian Quakers*, Oxford, 1970

Kelleher, M.D. and Kelleher, C.L.: *Murder most rare: the female serial killer*, Dell, 1999

Kesselring, Joseph: *Arsenic and old lace*, Josef Weinberger, 2002

Lattimore, Richmond (trans.) *The Odyssey of Homer*, Harper, 1975

Levi, Primo: *The periodic table*, Penguin, 2000

Levy, Joel: *Poison: A social history*, Quid, 2011

Marriner, Brian: *Forensic clues to murder*, Arrow, 1991

Milburn, Geoffrey and Miller, Stuart T: *Sunderland: river, town and people*, Borough of Sunderland, 1988

Patterson, James: *A guide to Sunderland*, Hills & Co., 1897

Peacock, Tom: *Bygone Blucher & North Walbottle*, Newcastle City Libraries & Arts, 1994

Shakespeare, William: *Measure for measure*, Arden, 1967

Thomas, Donald: *The Victorian underworld*, John Murray, 1999

Vernon, Virginia: *Enchanting little lady*, Abelard-Schuman, 1964

Webb, Simon: *The Prince Bishops of Durham*, The Langley Press, 2011

Webb, Simon: *Victorian Durham*, The Langley Press, 2010

Whitehead, Tony: *Mary Ann Cotton: Dead, but not forgotten*, Tony Whitehead, 2000

Whorton, James C.: *The arsenic century*, Oxford, 2009

Wingate, Peter with Wingate, Richard: *The Penguin medical encyclopaedia*, Penguin, 1988

ALSO FROM THE LANGLEY PRESS:

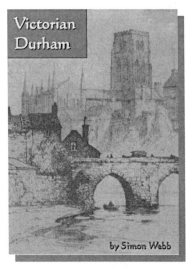